Conformity

Conformity

CHARLES A. KIESLER
Yale University
and
SARA B. KIESLER
Connecticut College

ADDISON-WESLEY PUBLISHING COMPANY
Reading, Massachusetts
Menlo Park, California · London · Don Mills, Ontario

TOPICS IN SOCIAL PSYCHOLOGY
Charles A. Kiesler, Yale University, Series Editor

To TINA and THOMAS KIESLER
for their patience

Foreword

It is becoming increasingly difficult for anyone to be a generalist in social psychology. Not only is the number of articles published zooming, but new researchable areas of interest are multiplying as well. A researcher finds more fascinating topics these days than he used to, but he also finds himself behind in his reading of all but one or two of them. As a result, the quality of the broad introductory book in social psychology has suffered. No one can any longer be an expert in all of social psychology.

As an alternative, we offer the present series, *Topics in Social Psychology*, directed toward the student with no prior background in social psychology. Taken as a whole, the series adequately covers the field of social psychology, but it has the advantage that each short book was written by an expert in the area. The given instructor can select some subset of the books to make up his course, the particular subset depending upon his biases and inclinations. In addition, the individual volumes could be useful in several ways: as supplementary reading in, perhaps, a sociology course; to introduce more advanced courses (for example, a graduate seminar in attitude change); or just for peeking at recent developments in social psychology.

The present volume, authored by my wife and myself, is concerned with the problem of conformity—what it means and when it happens. In considering this problem, one of social influence, we had to consider several related issues, such as the effects of the mere presence of others on us, communication within groups, and so forth. One of the main points of the book is a distinction between compliance (or going along with the group) and private acceptance (really changing one's opinion as a result of interaction with the group).

Charles A. Kiesler

Contents

CHAPTER ONE

The Nature of Conformity and Its Investigation

If you had been reading a newspaper in a particular city in the Northern United States in late September of 1954, you might have seen a back-page headline reading: "PROPHECY FROM PLANET. CLARION CALL TO CITY: FLEE THAT FLOOD. IT'LL SWAMP US ON DEC. 21, OUTER SPACE TELLS SUBURBANITE." The item had been supplied by a "Mrs. Keech," who maintained that the prophecy was not her own. She said that she had received many messages by automatic writing, sent to her by superior beings from a planet called "Clarion." The beings, who had visited the earth in flying saucers, had noticed fault lines in the earth's crust that foretold the deluge. Mrs. Keech reported that the flood would spread from the Arctic Circle to the Gulf of Mexico. At the same time, she said, a cataclysm would engulf the West Coast from Seattle to Chile.

Mrs. Keech had gathered about her a number of followers who also believed in the prophecy and were preparing for the great event. When no flood appeared on December 21, many of the group left. However, the people most committed to the prophecy not only persisted in their beliefs after disconfirmation, but started to recruit new believers and group members.

Several psychologists and their students seized this opportunity to study what happens to people when their beliefs are disconfirmed, and they observed Mrs. Keech and her unusual group of followers over a period of months. Some, pretending to be believers, even joined the group. Their research was reported in a book called *When Prophecy Fails* (Festinger, Riecken, and Schachter, 1956).* This detailed report describes a number of

---

*References are listed at the end of the book.

activities and attitudes which can be subsumed under the heading of *conformity*. Examples from the prophecy group will be used throughout this chapter to illustrate various aspects of conformity.

DEFINING CONFORMITY

Conformity as Change toward a Group

Whether we are discussing the "true believer," ourselves, or the man in the street, conformity is defined in the same way: *a change in behavior or belief toward a group as a result of real or imagined group pressure.* We will first discuss what we mean by "change toward a group."

Everyone belongs to groups of people. Moreover, these groups influence us. Our behavior and attitudes change as we interact with others. A group will want an individual member to act and believe as the others do. Consequently, the end result of group influence is that our beliefs and actions will be more similar to those of others in the group. Sometimes one member of our group will influence us more than others. For example, the leader of a group, or a united clique within the group, may be more influential than other members. Of course, any member of a group may be influenced by any of the others. If each member influences others and is influenced himself, the members will become more and more like each other in attitude and action. In many groups, then, each member of a group changes his attitudes and actions to be more like those of the others, and, overall, the group becomes more uniform in belief and behavior.

It won't happen quite like this for all people, of course. If you belong to a group in name only, the members may not influence you at all. Or if you belong to a group only because you have to (say, your parents insist that you join a club for which you have no affection), then you may resist all influence attempts. We have simply described what *can* happen as a result of membership in a group.

Mrs. Keech's group illustrates our conformity paradigm quite well. Here was a conglomeration of friends, married couples, and strangers who just seemed to happen along, all brought together because of some attraction or another to Mrs. Keech and the activities she was engaged in. There was a core membership of fifteen persons and a few others who drifted in and out. Some of the members of the group, especially the two leaders, Mrs. Keech and a Dr. Armstrong, entered the group with a common set of beliefs: belief in extrasensory perception, in the spirit world, in reincarnation, and in the possibility of communication with outer space beings. Mrs. Keech convinced the other members of the imminence of the great flood. But the process of change did not stop there.

The members who met with Mrs. Keech and Dr. Armstrong were constantly cajoled or more subtly pressured into believing and acting more as their leaders expected. At group meetings, the members were asked to discuss their mystical experiences and dreams so that their "correct" meanings could be found. (This proved to be a little embarrassing for the researching infiltrators.) The group prayed together for common guidance and in doing so they tried to adjust their "vibrations" so that they would be in tune with each other. Newcomers to the group were given lessons by the more committed (one of the less subtle persuasive techniques); individuals who outwardly refused to accept the major beliefs (e.g., belief in ESP) were rejected or suspected of spying.

These techniques were rather successful in influencing the membership, at least before the disconfirmation of the prophecy. The beliefs of group members became more like those of the leaders, and the activities and attitudes of all the members became more and more uniform. Even after disconfirmation, the members most committed to the group continued to conform to the group's standards of belief and behavior.

These events illustrate what the study of conformity is directed at: changes in belief and behavior that a member of a group may undergo as a result of pressure from one or more other members of the group. We may also want to study how the combined changes of members result in group uniformity, how persistent the changes are, and what further changes take place when the circumstances are different. Of course, we are not interested in just any change. When we study conformity, we study change *toward the group*, i.e., movement in beliefs and behavior that make them more like those of other group members.

The Compliant Skeptic versus the True Believer

Not all of Mrs. Keech's circle really believed in her prophecy. There were some (including the spying researchers) who were skeptical, but who nevertheless had other reasons for acting as the group expected and demanded. Both kinds of people—the compliant skeptics and the true believers—were conformers, since they both displayed some sort of change in the direction of group expectations. However, it should be obvious that we must make some distinction between these two kinds of conformity.

Social psychologists have labeled these two types of conformity *compliance* and *private acceptance*. Compliance refers to overt behavior which becomes more like the behavior that the group wishes its members to show. The term refers to outward actions without consideration of the private convictions of the actor. When we speak of "compliance only," we mean that the person is behaving as the group wants him to but does not really believe in what he is doing. That is, he is going along with the group without privately agreeing with the group. Private acceptance means a change in attitude or belief in the direction of group attitudes and beliefs. In this case, the person may not only act as the group wishes, but changes his opinions so that he believes as the group believes. This term has its parallel in the term "attitude change" used in studies of persuasive communications.

Two members of Mrs. Keech's group can be used to illustrate the difference between compliance and private acceptance. Cleo Armstrong was the "compliant skeptic." She was the college-age daughter of two of the most committed members of the group. Her father was Dr. Armstrong, whom we have described as one of the leaders of the group. Because of her parents, Cleo was "stuck" with the group. At times she remarked that she had a great deal to lose if the flood prediction were not confirmed because of the community's certain resultant disrespect for her father. Thus she participated in the meetings and discussions, and never openly denied a belief in the prophecy. In all outward respects she conformed with the group. Yet her private convictions wavered a great deal. She did not proselytize on her own, she devoted little effort to studying Mrs. Keech's mimeographed lessons, and she argued extensively with her father. Cleo Armstrong, then, showed outward compliance without much private acceptance of the group's belief system.

Bob Eastman was a "true believer." He had once been a cynical, hard-living individual, who, after a stint in the Army, had entered college. He had come under the tutorship of Dr. Armstrong and became his faithful disciple. Eastman attended every meeting of the group; gave up smoking, drinking, and swearing; studied the lessons on his own; and worked hard in a secretarial capacity for the group. He sold property to pay off his debts before the flood, said goodbye to his parents after failing to convince them of the imminent catastrophe, and actively proselytized other students. He seemed to believe completely in the prophecy. By our definition, he displayed compliance with the group's norms and private acceptance of them.

Although both compliance and private acceptance are subsumed under the general notion of conformity, the conditions under which each occurs may be quite different. This is one reason why we have partitioned our later discussion into separate chapters on compliance and private acceptance. Also, most studies in the psychological literature have employed either measures of compliance or measures of private acceptance, but rarely both together. This historical fact is perhaps unfortunate because it would be of interest to examine how the two types of conformity interact. For example, we might want to examine the conditions under which private acceptance occurs but not overt compliance. Perhaps this occurs when it is easy for a person to change his beliefs but difficult to behave as the group does. For example, a smoker thinking of quitting may join a "smoking clinic" and be persuaded that to stop smoking is extremely important but still find it very hard to act on this belief.

Compliance and private acceptance may also have different psychological implications. Take, for example, the complier. The person who outwardly complies with the group but does not privately accept the group's beliefs is doing this for one or more of a number of reasons. Perhaps he thinks others will look up to him if he acts as the group does, as when a draftee walks down the street in that certain manner we call "military bearing." Perhaps the complier thinks the group will get him where he wants to go, as with the debutante who hates coming-out parties, but thinks if she attends them she may find a rich husband. Maybe he complies because he is forced to, as with the prisoner who labors diligently all day. Compliant behavior, itself, has implications for subsequent events. The person may feel a need to justify to himself what he is doing, so he may exaggerate the importance of his "motive" for complying, or he may eventually decide that he really does believe in what he is doing; or, upon examining his behavior, he may decide (if he can) to quit the group altogether. What happens will depend upon the situation: the extent to which the person is stuck with the group, the pressures on him to comply, and so forth.

Sometimes a complier never comes to the point where he feels the need to examine his behavior. Perhaps he well knows that he was forced to act as he is acting, or maybe the behavior is too insignificant in his life to bother with. In the case where the person feels he has no choice in behaving as he does, he will probably stop complying the minute the group turns its back or releases its hold on him.

The psychological implications of private acceptance may be very different. The person who believes in what he does will probably persist in his behavior long after the group has stopped monitoring his behavior—as long, in fact, as he continues to believe. When the person considers what he is doing, he thinks, "I'm doing these things because I believe in them." Further actions on the issue will be dictated by his belief. The person may also change other attitudes to bring them in line with his new belief.

In addition, private acceptance is likely to intensify the person's relationship to the other group members, since he feels similar to them in belief as well as action. If the group is ideologically attacked, he may defend it. (After all, when the group's beliefs are attacked, so are his.) In a sense, a person who privately accepts the group's beliefs has a greater investment in the group. Not only is he likely to devote more time and effort to its activities, but these efforts are whole-hearted. The group has far more potential influence in other areas of his life than if he were only complying.

On the other hand, we cannot conclude that the person who changes his beliefs will always increase his affection for the group more than the person who just complies. We mentioned above that the complier may need to justify his behavior because it is discrepant with his beliefs. When he asks himself, "Why am I doing these things?", he cannot say, ". . . because I believe in them." Consequently, he may attempt to justify his behavior by increasing his liking for the group. He says, "I do these things, even though I don't believe, because the group members are marvelous people." The person who acts out of private conviction does not have to justify his behavior, so he may be less likely to increase his attention to the group. We shall later discuss in some detail when the complier will be a more enthusiastic group member. To sort out the differential predictions, we have to know more about the conditions under which compliance and private acceptance occur. Let it suffice to know that the person may be in an entirely different psychological situation, depending on whether he has complied overtly or has privately changed his beliefs.

Measuring Compliance and Private Acceptance

We mentioned before that, historically, few studies have employed measures of both compliance and private acceptance. The techniques for studying compliance and private acceptance usually require very different strategies, and to combine the two in the same experiment would be quite difficult. By understanding how the two kinds of conformity are investigated, the implications of the distinction between them will become clearer.

We can more or less readily observe whether or not a person overtly complies with a particular group demand. It is a little more difficult to find out if the same person privately accepts group influence, since we cannot directly observe his private, personal opinions. Psychologists who studied compliance in the past ordinarily exposed people to group influence attempts and then, with the group still around, simply waited to see if the individuals copied the group's example. When interest in private acceptance grew, psychologists learned that this method was inadequate, so they devised more subtle methods for investigating private acceptance. Sometimes they exposed people to group influence and then withdrew the group so that they could observe their subjects when the group was no longer present. Sometimes they kept the group intact, but let members express their opinions on anonymous questionnaires.

A classic study of compliance. The method in this study was first employed by Solomon Asch. A number of confederates, after being told what to do beforehand, participate with a naive subject who thinks they are also subjects. Suppose we have four confederates. They enter the experiment room with the subject and sit in a semicircle with the subject forced to take an end seat. The experimenter tells the group that they will make judgments of a series of lines. They are to compare one line with three others and choose the one of the same length (see Fig. 1-1). The confederates, instead of choosing the line which obviously matches the comparison line, choose one of a different length. The subject is then in a dilemma: should he identify the correct line, or should he yield to social pressure and pick the line the others chose? Two measures of compliance in this situation could be the number of subjects who pick the incorrect line and the number of trials on which subjects yield.

 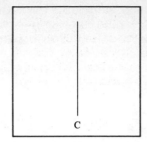

Fig. 1-1. A sample judgmental stimulus used in Asch-type studies of compliance.

A number of independent variables can be studied in this type of experimental setting. For example, if we are interested in the effect of group size on conformity, we can vary the number of confederates. If we are interested in the effect of status, we can vary the status of the confederates by introducing them differently or by having them wear different clothes.

The Asch technique allows us to study compliance under a number of different conditions. But we have no way of knowing what the subjects are privately thinking. Do they actually come to believe that the line the confederates chose is the correct line? Not often. One line and only one line is correct, even though the others say it isn't. No matter how the subject squirms and squints, he cannot make their choice look correct. Thus, there is no room for private acceptance in this situation.

Now let's shorten the longest line and lengthen the shortest one until it really isn't too clear which is correct. The situation then becomes ambiguous enough so that the subject's private opinion might indeed by swayed by the confederates. Could we measure private acceptance by perhaps having him whisper his answer to the experimenter? Probably not. The subject might guess that conformity was the experimenter's real interest. If a subject guesses the real purpose of an experiment, we cannot depend on his response. If he were to tell the experimenter that he privately agreed with the confederates, we wouldn't know if he actually did or if he just wished to please the experimenter. If he told the experimenter that he disagreed with the confederates, he might only be trying to convince the experimenter that he was an independent sort of person. For the same reasons, an anonymous questionnaire would be inadequate. Without any rationale for the questionnaire, the subject would still wonder what the purpose of the experiment was. Originally, the subject was involved in what he thought was a judgmental task. But when we ask him to repeat his judgment, either on a questionnaire or by whispering to the experimenter, he becomes suspicious. The situation is both artifical and unbelievable. In short, it is difficult to measure private acceptance with the Asch technique. It is not even clear that the Asch technique provides an adequate measure of compliance.

In recent years, psychologists have discovered that if they really want to study conformity—both private acceptance *and* compliance—they must be far more subtle. This subtlety requires that: (1) the experimenter not reveal his hypothesis to the subject (called "experimenter demand," because a revealed hypothesis puts pressure on the subject to satisfy it); (2) the experimental situation not be so contrived that the results cannot be generalized to other situations; and (3) the situation not be so artificial that the subject reacts suspiciously or defensively rather than as he would if the same variables were operating naturally. These considerations are taken into account in the following example of a study of private acceptance.

A hypothetical study of private acceptance. Suppose a person has never thought one way or the other about why he brushes his teeth. He just does it. He participates in our experiment with some confederates who discuss toothbrushing under the guise of a seminar on "cultural truisms." The confederates take the position that toothbrushing is actually harmful to the teeth (it wears down the enamel) and should be substituted by rinsing with a mouthwash. To measure compliance, we can observe whether the subject overtly agrees with the confederates.

Overt agreement, however, would not indicate private acceptance. A more complicated technique is required. One reasonable method would be to use another subject who also is exposed to the group but is never asked to express his opinion. We will measure his opinion later. (There are two reasons why we do not ask the subject to express his opinion in the group. First, this might make him suspicious when we later measure his opinion, and second, the act of complying, itself, might affect his private acceptance of the group's opinion.) Later, he is asked to participate in another experiment. In the second experiment, a new experimenter tells him that the study is concerned with "reading skills" and that his reading speed and comprehension will be tested. Among the materials he reads is a persuasive communication (say, from the "Dental Institute") which advocates brushing the teeth three times a day. An anonymous questionnaire (the "comprehension test") is then given to the subject. Imbedded among several questions is one which asks, "How often should a person brush his teeth?" If the subject had been convinced by the discussion group that toothbrushing is harmful, he should be more resistant to the communication than would a control subject who had not participated in the discussion group. That is, the experimental subject should be more likely to answer that one should rarely brush one's teeth. But if the subject had not been convinced by the group, then both he and the control subject should be influenced by the communication. They might answer that one must brush his teeth two or three times a day. Thus, one way to measure private acceptance is to see whether the subject still endorses the group's opinion after attack.

The experiment outlined above illustrates some important problems in defining conformity. First, the behavior of interest must be precisely described so that it can be measured. In particular, it is essential to distinguish between behavior that merely goes along with the group's and behavior reflecting true agreement with the group. Second, measures of conformity must be taken within a context that is believable to the subject.

Does One Have to Change in Order to Conform?

The answer to our subtitle is that it depends partly on how one defines conformity. However, conformity could not be defined to include behavior that just happened to coincide with that of a group because behavior that is truly coincidental has nothing to do with the psychological effect of a group. Conformity, as we have defined it, involves an alteration of behavior and belief toward a group. It is not just any alteration—it is alteration that occurs as a result of some group pressure. If a person agrees with a group just by coincidence, we would not call this conformity. Let us examine this notion more thoroughly.

Conformity was clearly demonstrated in the behavior of Kitty O'Donnell, one of Mrs. Keech's prophecy group. She first came to a meeting at Bob Eastman's urging. At first, she considered the group a "bunch of crackpots." But she consented to listen to what the group had to say. Later, she had a dream which convinced her she had been "chosen" to be one of the group. Eventually, she accepted the group's beliefs and plunged herself into group activities, quit her job, and left her parents' home. She obviously changed toward the group's beliefs. It was not a coincidental agreement with the group, nor even a chance movement toward the group. The group had an effect on her. Kitty O'Donnell illustrates our definition of conformity: a change toward the group as a result of real (or imagined) group pressure.

To illustrate coincidental agreement let us suppose that a person in India had consulted the stars and decided that on December 21 a great flood would appear on the American continent. However, he had never heard of Mrs. Keech and knew nothing of her group. We would not call him a conformer, even though he came to believe as Mrs. Keech and her group did. She and her group did not influence him (unless one believes in ESP). Regardless of the fascinating coincidence, his behavior is psychologically irrelevant when we are studying the effect of Mrs. Keech and her co-believers.

We have limited our definition of conformity to changes in belief and behavior as a result of group pressure. But a bright student may still make the point that one can be interested in the effect of group pressure without necessarily confining oneself to change. What if a person were in a group, happened to agree with its standards before he joined, but *maintained* his beliefs as a result of group pressure? What follows is an example from the Keech group.

Dr. Armstrong was a physician working on the staff of a college health service. He and his wife were active in religious organizations and Dr. Armstrong organized "The Seekers," a group of young people who met weekly to discuss various topics, including one of Dr. Armstrong's favorites, flying saucers. He joined with Mrs. Keech because they were of like mind. The group did not change him—he already had a set of beliefs consistent with Mrs. Keech's prophecy. However, it is possible that without the constant presence of Mrs. Keech and the group Dr. Armstrong may have reverted to a more conventional belief system. Can we not, then, speak of his conformity?*

Why don't we say that maintenance of a belief in a group is also conformity? Because without other information, we cannot demonstrate that the group had any effect on the person. We would know that the individual, like Dr. Armstrong, did not abandon his beliefs while in the group, but we would not know that the group caused the belief maintenance. Perhaps the belief would have remained intact without the group. However, there is one instance when belief maintenance can be called conformity. That is when comparable people outside the group abandon their opinions. In this case, by proper comparison with these control subjects, one could conclude that the group made the individual resistant to change—he would have held a different opinion had he not been in the group. Since the control subjects alter their opinions and those in the group do not, the difference between them represents a change, albeit an indirect one. In a sense, the difference between the two conditions reflects the change in the group member that would have occurred without group support. This argument is analogous to the one presented in our previous discussion of how to measure private acceptance.

Let us summarize our point. In research on conformity, we are forced to examine change, directly or by inference, to be assured that the group has had some effect on the individual. This is why we limit our definition of conformity to changes in belief and behavior toward a group. There are two main ways to examine this change. Sometimes we compare subjects' behavior after group interaction with the behavior of other subjects who were not in the group. A difference between them allows us to infer change. A second method is to expose both of these groups of subjects to an attack on their beliefs. Again, we can infer change by comparing relative resistance

---

*Some psychologists (e.g., Hollander and Willis, 1967) call this "congruence conformity," as opposed to "movement conformity," which we have been discussing.

to attack in the two subject groups. Both methods allow us to conclude whether the group has had an effect on the person, in short, whether conformity had occurred.

Conformity to What?

As we mentioned previously, a person belongs to many groups. In an uncontrolled setting, it can be very misleading to restrict oneself to an examination of a person's behavior with respect to only one group or to one situation. If we fail to analyze the whole psychological environment, we may eventually draw the wrong conclusions. That is, we may infer that a particular variable was influencing the person when actually something quite different may have caused him to change his behavior.

Say we are interested in the effect of parental attitudes on the behavior of children. As a small study, we might correlate the dating behavior of teenagers with the "permissiveness" of their parents. Permissiveness is defined as few restrictions on behavior. Suppose we find that teenagers with permissive parents are more frequent daters than teenagers with nonpermissive parents. Can we conclude that the permissive parents want their children to date more and have influenced them to do so? We cannot. Perhaps the children of permissive parents, because the parents dictate less of their behavior, become more dependent on their peers. If frequent dating is positively valued in the teenage culture, the children might as easily be conforming to teenage norms as to parental norms, if they are conforming at all. In short, only with more information about the whole context of the behavior could we draw any conclusion about conformity.

Conformity as a Personality Trait

The layman often thinks of conformity as a personality trait: there are the conformers and then there are the nonconformers. Whether the layman thinks of himself as a conformer or not may depend upon whom he is comparing himself to. If he is considering himself relative to those he considers beatniks, hippies, or bums, he is a staunch conformer—he is not, in his own eyes, one of those awful nonconformers who are likely to reject Mother, God, and Country all at once. However, if he is asked if he believes in "changes for the better" (whatever they are), he will suddenly assume that he is a brave nonconformer, unshackled by the inhibitions and fears of the old fogies. While we often are attracted by the idea of conformity as an enduring personality trait, we may be unwilling to accept it in ourselves.

A number of psychologists are interested in conformity as a personality trait, but complete discussion of this topic is beyond the scope of this book. We will limit ourselves to presenting two major pitfalls that one may encounter if he assumes that conformity is a personality trait.

The first pitfall has already been hinted at in our discussion of the layman's psychology of conformity. That is, by labeling people as "conformers" and "nonconformers" we may be encouraged to let value judgments intrude into our thinking. Take Mrs. Keech's group again. We have seen how Mrs. Keech convinced her followers of the outlandish flood prophecy—or if not convinced, got them to cooperate in her spiritual ventures. Why were these people willing to go along with such notions? One argument might be that these were "weak" persons who were influenced because of their acquiescent personalities. This hypothesis is not objective since it ignores the parallels between the behavior of Mrs. Keech's disciples and our own behavior (as when we copy the dress styles of our peers or the political opinions of our parents).

A second problem with the idea that conformity reflects an acquiescent or "conformer" personality is that this explanation is no explanation at all. All it really says is that conformers conform. But why do they conform? Do they conform in every situation? Obviously not, for some of Mrs. Keech's group left in disillusionment when the prophecy failed. The argument that these people were *more* prone to conformity than the rest of us, had more acquiescent or conforming personalities, is not very helpful either. For one thing, one could argue that the members of the prophecy group were *less* conformist than most of us, because they did not accept many of the beliefs that the rest of our society holds. That is, they did not conform to the majority idea of the pragmatic, realistic, "objective" American, who goes to a conventional church and would never accept such a fatalistic prophecy. Again we must ask, conformity to what? They were conforming to their group, but we conform to ours. For the long-range goal of finding out why people conform, labels are not profitable.

A Note on Group Pressure

We repeat our definition of conformity: conformity is a change in behavior or belief toward a group as a result of real or imagined group pressure. We have not yet discussed the phrase, "as a result of real or imagined group pressure." We have, however, emphasized that we are interested in changes that occur due to the group. Group pressure refers to the process by which the group seeks to impose its influence on the person. Group pressure is sometimes an explicit attempt by group members to impose standards on the person, but not always. All that is required is that the group expect the person to act or believe in a certain way, or that that person think such things are expected of him. The whole process by which group pressure is exerted is reserved for the next chapter, where we discuss the concept of group in more detail.

RESEARCH IN CONFORMITY

It is not enough, even in an introductory text, simply to define conformity as we have done and then review what is known about its causes. The reader should also be made familiar with how one researches the area. There are two major reasons why a student should know how research is conducted.

First, a number of observations have been made by researchers which still need interpretation if we are to make generalizations about conformity. Here is a hypothetical example. Say one researcher found that when the "Pineapple Republic" was at war, the people apparently conformed to its leaders' demands more than in peacetime. Another researcher, however, found the opposite when observing the "Pear Republic." Naturally, the situations under which the war was begun would make a big difference, as would the past history of the nation, the type of leadership provided, and so forth. We must be aware of all these data, but we also need to know how the observations were made and under what conditions in order to start interpreting the evidence and reaching some conclusions. Let us say that the first researcher asked the leaders themselves how much the people agreed with their policies. (Say he did this because the Pineapple Republic was a dictatorship where polling was not allowed.) They said the people were conforming more than in peacetime. The second researcher, being a member of a polling company in the U.S.A., asked a random sample of citizens in the Pear Republic how much they agreed with their leaders' goals. The results of the poll showed that before the war people agreed more than during the war.

Now that we know how the research was conducted in the two studies, we can weigh the evidence concerning the conflicting conclusions which were drawn. It is obvious that the evidence is not clear. The opposite interpretations that the researchers came to probably had more to do with their methods than with their observations. Often, to explain data, we must know how they were gathered.

A second reason for knowing how to do research is that one will then know how to pose questions which can be answered empirically. For example, we mentioned earlier that one must measure changes in behavior in order to find out if a group has had an effect on a person. Clearly, questions concerning why conformity occurs must be phrased in such a way that we can observe change. Here is another example. Suppose we are interested in the effect of a new beer commercial. By knowing how to investigate this problem empirically, we know what questions can be asked in the first place. We would realize that the question "Does the commercial have an effect?" is much too imprecise. In the course of your life you will be asking many questions about your own or others' observations, and you will be hearing the questions (and answers) that others pose. One should be able to evaluate questions and know how they could be answered empirically.

The student should understand how an experiment is conducted. As an aid, we will describe in detail a hypothetical experiment in conformity. We will also discuss why the particular procedures were used and some other ways of going about the same task.

An Experiment on Cheating

You have a friend, say, who reports the following incident. He had just taken two final examinations. Despite his anxiety and fatigue during these ordeals, he noticed a curious event. During the first examination, a student walked in with a sheaf of notes hidden in his books. After sneaking into a rear seat, he began the exam. Soon after, he furtively glanced around the room, drew out his notes, and—hunching over—made use of them on the examination. Your friend was sure that almost everyone taking the exam was aware of the student's cheating. They also could have cheated by simply picking up their own notes and books and using them, but no one did so. Your friend forgot the incident until the second examination. In that exam, he also saw a student cheat, but this time the student strolled into the exam late, brandished his notes in the air, and sat at the front of the room. Settling into his chair with a flourish, he smiled at the others around him and began to cheat. Then, several other students began to follow his example, and, before the hour was up, half of the class had cheated. Your friend wants to know why no one imitated the cheater in the first examination and why so many did in the second examination.

Generating hypotheses. Perhaps this example does not precisely fit our definition of conformity, since students are imitating an individual rather than a group. However, a person's actions are often taken to reflect his group's norms. So let us assume for the sake of exposition that we have an instance of conformity. Some students in the second examination presumably changed from noncheaters into cheaters because of the presence of a cheater in their midst. But this happened only in the second examination. To find out why, we should begin by analyzing the differences between the first situation and the second. A relatively simple explanation is that many more students must have noticed the second cheater than the first because of the obvious way the second was acting. That is, perhaps more students cheated the second time because more had watched the cheater and thus had the idea to do it. Another simple explanation could lie in the value of cheating. If the first examination was one which called for interpretations of historical events and the second for reproductions of dates and places, then cheating may have been more widespread in the latter case only because copying from notes was more profitable there. Finally, one could argue that the friend didn't really notice how much cheating was going on in the first examination and that it wasn't until the second examination that he was really looking for it.

These explanations are obvious: one can't imitate cheating unless he sees someone cheat and one probably wouldn't cheat unless he could benefit by it. If we could control the situation so that every student noticed the cheater, and if we could keep the examination the same, perhaps we would still find a difference. Let's look for a more interesting explanation. For example, your friend might think the reason everyone cheated in the second exam was because the second cheater acted with so much flair and élan. People prefer to follow a person with style and self-confidence. Nobody wants to copy a person who sneaks around and looks frightened and ashamed. Our experiment has been designed to test this hypothesis.

Experimental design. The question "Does a cheater's élan influence the extent to which others in his group cheat?" may be researchable. We know exactly what we are looking for: an increase in cheating by group members after they observe someone cheat. We know also that we can take the situation into a laboratory where obvious variables (as the physical opportunity to cheat) can be controlled. We might use three groups of subjects. One experimental group could observe a cheater (a confederate) acting with élan. Another experimental group could observe the cheater acting without élan. A third control group could observe the confederate when he did not cheat.

If subjects in each group cheated about equally, then we would conclude that having a cheater serve as an example had no particular effect on the subjects. If the two experimental groups cheated equally but both groups cheated more than the control group did, we would conclude that the confederate cheater induced cheating. However, there would be no evidence that the élan of the cheater had any effect on the subjects. Only if the élan experimental group cheated more than the other two groups, could we say that the cheater's élan was influential in determining the extent to which subjects cheated.

Is this the best experiment we could do? Perhaps not. To see the wisdom of this, we must look again at our élan hypothesis. A social psychologist would ask why élan contributes to compliance. Certainly we are better off testing *why* it works as well as *if* it works—and these can be tested at the same time. By finding out why élan has the effects it does, we will be better able to predict its effects in other situations. For example, if élan helps to induce compliance because it makes people like the person with that quality, then we will know that liking for a model is the necessary ingredient to get compliance rather than élan *per se*. We could then predict that when élan is displayed in a boastful or hateful way, compliance should decrease rather than increase.

Why might élan induce compliance? We can think of several possibilities, and perhaps you can conjure up even more. (1) Perhaps a person with
élan seems so self-confident that he makes those around him anxious and
increasingly unsure that what they are doing is best. If so, they might look
to him for a better way of behaving. By conforming to his example, they
might regain their self-confidence. In examinations, students are already
somewhat anxious. When another student strolls in and cheats with obvious
pleasure, they may be shaken up a bit. Are they doing the right thing? When
they cheat as he does, they at least know that they are doing what this
self-confident person thinks is right. (2) Maybe the person who cheats with
élan redefines the situation for students as one where cheating is less risky
than they thought before. After all, the cheater seems to know exactly what
he is doing. He would not act like that if he thought he were going to be
caught the next minute (or, if caught, punished severely). So perhaps élan
has its effect by reducing the perceived risk of cheating. (3) It is possible, as
we noted earlier, that a person who acts with élan is a likable person. When
someone has flair and self-confidence, we assume that he knows his way
around the world, that he is used to achievement and success, perhaps that
he is of high social and economic status. We tend to admire and like those
with high prestige value, and moreover we tend to imitate them. Therefore,
the cheater with élan may induce compliance because he seems to be a
prestigious and likable person.

We have arbitrarily chosen one of these hypotheses to test experimentally. The experiment outlined below tests the hypothesis that the élan of a
model induces compliance when it reduces the perceived risk of complying.
However, we must design our experiment with all the hypotheses in mind so
that the two other hypotheses can be ruled out when we interpret our data.
The results must not be interpretable in terms of the subject's anxiety or his
respect for the cheater. This can be accomplished by manipulating perceived
risk independently of élan to see its special contribution to conformity. We
are interested, then, in testing the interactive effect of two independent
variables: a model's élan and perceived risk. Our dependent variable is the
overt cheating behavior of subjects.

We have conceptually separated our independent variables, but we must
also experimentally separate them. In psychological parlance, the variables
should be "orthogonally manipulated." To manipulate élan, we need a
model who can act in a manner which we operationally define as élan. Half
of the subjects will observe him. The other half of the subjects will observe
the same model, who cheats but without élan. Except for the élan
difference, the confederate must act exactly the same way for each subject.
To accomplish this, we will use a video tape of his behavior.

To manipulate the perceived risk of compliance, we could do several
things. We could vary how scared the model seemed of possible punishment
(by having him look at the proctor a lot or a little, say). But this would not
do because how scared he looked might affect our perception of how much

élan he has. We want to make this manipulation independent of the first. A better way would be to let the subjects know in advance what the actual risks of cheating were. We will vary the possiblility of getting caught. If élan of a cheater is effective because it makes the risks of cheating seem low, then our experimental results should show that élan affected compliance only when the risk was not clearly high. If our hypothesis has merit, the subject should not cheat, even when the model has élan, when he knows that cheating will be swiftly discovered and punished. We suggest, then, that prior to his exposure to the model, the subject be given an independent appraisal of his chances for successful cheating. The completed experimental design is shown in Table 1-1.

TABLE 1-1

An Experiment on Cheating Behavior: Cheating as a Function of the "Élan" of a Model and the Perceived Risk of Cheating

		Behavior of Model	
		Élan	No Élan
Perceived Risk of Cheating	High Perceived Risk	1*	1
	Moderate Perceived Risk	4	2

*Predicted compliance effects, on scale from 1-4, when 1 = least cheating and 4 = most cheating.

The design in Table 1-1 includes our predictions for compliance. Suppose we could rate the amount of cheating from 1 (least cheating) to 4 (most cheating). What do we expect in our various experimental conditions? We expect élan to have no effect when subjects are certain of being caught—subjects in neither élan condition would cheat. Élan should increase cheating (as compared to no élan) *only* when the risks of cheating are lower.

Table 1-1 shows three levels of risk. Why have the low risk conditions? Actually, they serve as control groups. Suppose they were left out. Any increase in cheating by those in the élan-moderate risk condition might be attributed to several causes. (Can you think of some?) Our hypothesis says that élan affects cheating because it affects perceived risk. If so, élan should have little effect when the risk is small. On this basis, one would expect little difference between the two élan conditions when risk is low. Indeed, intuitively, one might guess that élan would even *decrease* cheating under low risk. That is, a model who acts with élan will seem to have too much bravado. Is he, perhaps, afraid? If this hunch is correct, one should obtain data arrayed as in our Table 1-1: élan having no effect when risk is high, increasing conformity with moderate risk, and reducing conformity when risk is low. (The table also shows that on the average, the less the risk, the greater the cheating—a rather obvious result.)

Procedure. To conduct the experiment, subjects must first be recruited. They can volunteer or be paid. However they are chosen, once they come to the experiment they must be randomly assigned to one of the six experimental conditions. In this experiment, there are several sessions, and six different subjects participate in each session. To ensure chance assignment we could randomly decide (using a table in a statistics book or picking slips out of a hat) what condition the whole group is to be assigned. A better way would be to have each experimental condition represented in a single session, again randomly deciding which subject is to be in which condition. The latter method controls perfectly for time of day, unplanned interruptions, and so forth.

The subjects, upon entering the experimental room, are seated in six separate cubicles outfitted with sound equipment and video screens. The experimenter introduces himself and tells the subjects that he is interested in the effect of "work conditions" on a person's performance. He explains that in his study he sometimes varies the lighting, sometimes the temperature of the room, sometimes the presence or absence of other people, and sometimes the task itself. He then tells the subjects that they will sometimes work alone in their cubicles and sometimes while their video screen is on so that they can see others working. They are told that they will perform various tasks, on which they should do as well as possible. For each correctly completed task, they will receive twenty-five cents (the object being to ensure some impetus to cheat). The experimenter tells all groups exactly the same thing.

The experimenter then turns on the video screen (to "demonstrate how it works") which seems alternately to scan the room and the other subjects. He excuses himself for a few minutes while he "gets the task materials in order." This begins the experiment. We constructed the rationale with an eye toward making the whole situation believable and realistic.

Why so much stress on believability and realism? Believability and realism ensure that the subject acts naturally and without suspicion. Imagine, for example, what might happen if the subject knew we were investigating compliance. We wouldn't know then whether he complied to please the experimenter or because of the independent variables. We could never generalize to a real-life situation where no experimenter was present.

We left our subjects waiting around for the experimenter. While they are waiting, we commence our manipulation of perceived risk. All subjects see on their video screen what looks like a conversation between the experimenter and a colleague. Actually, the conversation has been taped beforehand, as are all future video events. The manipulations are preprogrammed so that the experimenter is unaware to which condition each subject is assigned. This tactic prevents the experimenter from purposely or even unconsciously treating subjects differently and thereby possibly biasing the results (Rosenthal, 1963; Orne, 1962). To the subject, however, the camera seems to focus on the experimenter by chance. In each session, two subjects hear one conversation (the high risk manipulation), two hear another (the moderate risk manipulation), and two, a third (the low risk condition). The three conversations are practically identical. In fact, the manipulation is accomplished by varying only one word! Subjects hear the experimenter's friend ask, "How do you manage to watch all these kids at once? They can cheat, can't they?" In the high risk condition, the experimenter says, "Yes, but I catch them about 90% of the time. I report them if they do." In the moderate risk condition, he says, "Yes, but I catch them about 50% of the time. I report them if they do." In the low risk condition, the comparable percentage is 20%.

Notice how we have either ruled out or controlled for variables other than the one we wish to vary. The experimenter's manner or personality can have no systematic effect among conditions because all subjects see the same filmed experimenter (except for the single word which is spliced in). Other than riskiness, all subjects receive the same information. The subjects' own personalities will have no systematic effect because they are randomly assigned to experimental conditions. Finally, any differences among experimental sessions (e.g., time of day, laughter, etc.) cannot affect our results because each condition is represented at each session. Each of these variables could affect our results but not systematically. For example, the time of day that a session takes place will partly determine a subject's response to the manipulations. But since all conditions are represented in each session, the effect will not be systematic. It will affect one condition as much as another and could not result in differences between conditions.

After subjects hear the bogus conversation, the experimenter returns and gives each subject several tasks to work on. Each task is allotted a certain amount of time. During some of the tasks, the video is turned on; during others it is turned off. Midway in the tasks is a set of mathematical problems of great difficulty (to make cheating attractive), and while subjects work on them the video is scanning the "others" (remember that everything was taped beforehand). As if by chance, subjects see one of the other subjects turn to the back of the booklet where the answers are listed. To manipulate élan, half of the subjects see the confederate smile, lean back in his chair, and—whistling the whole time—copy the answers slowly and methodically without once looking around. The other half of the subjects see the same confederate copy the answers in the same way, but without smiling, leaning back, or whistling.

Each subject is now automatically photographed by the camera in his room. We want to see if our subjects will begin to cheat also. Afterwards we use the film to measure compliance in any one of several ways: (1) counting the number of subjects in each condition who copy answers, (2) counting the number of answers copied, and (3) measuring the time lapse between the model's cheating and the subjects' cheating.

When subjects complete the tasks, they are thanked by the experimenter and "debriefed." This means that the study is explained in detail and the true purposes of each part of the experiment are told. There are practical reasons for debriefing: subjects brought into the experimenter's confidence are unlikely to tell others about the experiment. Consequently, adequate debriefing leads to fewer suspicious future subjects. There are also ethical reasons for debriefing. It is unfair to our subjects, as people, to delude them—even in a minor way—and let them go away deluded. We must remove any psychological effect we might have had on them. Remember, we have induced some people to cheat. This must be discussed with subjects so that they walk out of the experiment no worse than they entered it. Debriefing is an important and delicate part of research. In many experiments, debriefing can take as long as the experiment itself.

Results. Our arbitrary measure of compliance is the percentage of subjects who cheat in each experimental condition. An examination of the differences among percentages enables an assessment of the relative effects of our independent variables. Suppose we find that about 20% of the subjects cheated in each of the two high risk conditions. This is what we expected: whether or not the confederate acts with flair, few should cheat when the risks of cheating are high. Turning now to the moderate risk conditions, say we find that when the model acted without élan, 30% cheated; when he acted with élan, 60% cheated. Suppose also that with risk low, 60% cheated under élan conditions, and 80% under no élan conditions (an average of 70%). These data tell us something about the effect of risk and the effect of élan. Let's ignore élan for a moment by averaging the risk conditions and comparing them with each other. Clearly, lowering the risk of cheating increased the frequency of cheating. That is, when risk was high, an average of 20% of the subjects cheated. But when the risk of cheating was moderate, an average of 45% cheated, i.e., (60% + 30%)/2. Under low risk, even more cheated.

Consider now the effect of élan. Élan increased cheating only when perceived risk was moderate. That is, when risk was moderate, more cheated when the model acted with élan than when he did not (60% versus 30%), but there was no difference when the risk was high (20% versus 20%), and even fewer cheated with the élan model when risk was low (60% versus 80%). Thus, imitative cheating depended on the combined effects of risk and the élan of a model. Only when risk was moderate, did élan heighten cheating (i.e., increase conformity). This type of effect is called an *interaction*, since one cannot explain the data without reference to both independent variables. The interaction allows us to conclude that our hypothesis has merit. That is, élan affects cheating only when the risk of cheating is not explicitly high. Presumably, if the subject knows that his chances for being caught are 90%, he will be unable to distort the situation, even if the model cheats with flair and self-confidence. He knows he will be caught. But if the subject thinks his chances for being caught are 50%, the model acting with élan may induce him to believe he can avoid notice. However, if the subject is aware of low risk anyway, flair has the opposite effect. It reduces cheating. Perhaps the model's behavior seems inappropriate and induces increased caution.

An interaction is particularly valuable in rejecting alternative explanations. Take, for example, the hypothesis that the élan of a model increases one's anxiety about the task and induces one to search for a more certain way of succeeding. This hypothesis predicts that subjects would cheat more when the confederate acted self-confidently. Obviously, the data do not match the prediction—élan increased cheating only when perceived risk was moderate. The same objection can be raised to the alternative hypothesis that élan increases cheating by raising the model's likability. The likability factor might not explain why élan increased cheating only when risk was moderate. Thus, interactions enable one to rule out alternative explanations by forcing one to consider the combined effects of more than one independent variable. The effect of one independent variable is readily explained in terms of a number of factors, whereas the interacting effects of two or more variables enable a more precise inference about the conditions under which a behavior is obtained.*

Measuring private acceptance. We tested the effects of a model's élan on compliance. What if we also wished to measure private acceptance, i.e., the conditions under which subjects valued cheating more, or thought cheating was a worthwhile activity? One way to measure private acceptance in our experiment would be to remove the subject from the group situation and see how he would behave in another, completely anonymous situation. We could ask each subject to report to another room. ("Since you have time left over, I wonder if you would do a favor for me. Another professor is compiling a questionnaire on student attitudes and needs help. He is down the hall.")

Each subject meets another experimenter. This second experimenter must remain ignorant of which experimental condition the subject was previously assigned. The "Student Attitudes" questionnaire is several pages long and asks the subject's opinion of a number of topics related to school (e.g., Do you prefer letter grades or number grades?). Imbedded in the

---

*This experiment is not perfect, by any means. For example, we never clearly defined élan. Moreover, the risk variable could be considered as simply a variation in constraint on the subject's ability to cheat. Nevertheless, we have chosen to present the experiment as we did because it provides, in a relatively simple manner, a general orientation toward research design and procedure.

STUDENT ATTITUDES

Instructions: Please place an arrow on each line to indicate your attitudes. Your arrow may be placed anywhere on the line.

1. How much do you agree that colleges should impose curfews on female students?

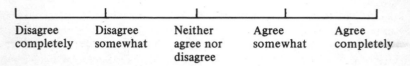

| Disagree completely | Disagree somewhat | Neither agree nor disagree | Agree somewhat | Agree completely |

2. To what extent is cheating on examinations justified in college?

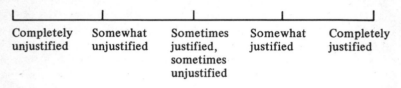

| Completely unjustified | Somewhat unjustified | Sometimes justified, sometimes unjustified | Somewhat justified | Completely justified |

3. . . .

Fig. 1-2.   A sample questionnaire.

questionnaire is our crucial question, "To what extent is cheating on examinations justified in college?" The subject answers by placing a mark on a scale designated at one end "Completely justified" and on the other "Completely unjustified" (see Fig. 1-2). When all subjects have completed the questionnaire, we arbitrarily assign numbers to each position on the scale, say 1 at one end and 100 at the other. (We can make a ruler to match the scale.) Each subject's score equals the number that is closest to his mark. The scores are summed and the mean score for each experimental condition is calculated. Then, the means are compared to see if private acceptance was differentially affected by our previous manipulations. That is, there should be differences among the six conditions if élan and risk had an effect on private acceptance. For example, there might be relatively high regard for cheating when risk was moderate and the confederate had élan.

Why did we use a different experimenter? The answer is that we wished to ensure that subjects answer honestly and naturally. If the first experimenter had given out the questionnaire, the subjects might have begun to question its purpose. "Why is he suddenly interested in student attitudes? Maybe he's really trying to see whether I'm a smart person or not. I notice the question on cheating. Maybe he's really doing research on that!" In other words, the subject given a questionnaire after manipulation may have "evaluation apprehension" (be afraid he's being evaluated: cf. Rosenberg, 1965), or may become sensitized to the crucial question. By separating a post-test from the experiment itself, these problems can be minimized.

Summary

We have described the experiment above, not so you can do an experiment on cheating, but so you can get an idea of how one does an experiment on conformity. Part of doing an experiment involves a "feel" for research For example, one must be able to put oneself in the subject's place and to see how the subject is perceiving the situation (remember our discussion of "conformity to what?"). Another part involves following certain rules of design, including random assignment of subjects to conditions making sure independent variables are actually manipulated independently of the others, etc. These rules enable one to evaluate the relationships of these data to his hypothesis. A third part involves planning ahead. For example, the experiment must be designed so that alternative explanations can either be rejected or ruled out. We hope this experiment gives you an idea of how to begin.

CHAPTER TWO

Group Pressure

Changes in belief or behavior can occur because a group puts psychological pressures on an individual to believe or act as it expects. These changes are called conformity. The previous chapter discussed the experimental study of change toward a group. This chapter is devoted to the concept of group pressure. An understanding of group pressure first requires a look at the notion of "group." We shall examine that concept; then we will turn to the problem of why people are involved in groups; finally, we will return to group pressure.

THE GROUP

To most laymen, a group is simply an aggregate of persons. Under this rubric is encompassed a wide range of collective bodies, from the U.S. Army to the social club. Social psychologists have discarded this definition because it is too broad to be very useful. *Social influence* is a general term for the many psychological effects that others have on the individual. It does not occur in all aggregates. The term "group" is usually reserved for those collections that have psychological implications for the individual. The definitional problem, then, lies in identifying when a collection has psychological implications for the individual, and which collections have them.

Social Influence in Aggregates

For centuries men have known that two or more individuals can affect each other psychologically. It was not until the 20th century, however, that anyone thoroughly and experimentally even tried to investigate these

24

effects. These sporadic attempts spawned social psychology. The result of this early research was a more sophisticated understanding of how people influence one another.

Floyd Allport was one of the first psychologists to study experimentally the effect of others on the individual. His early work illustrates what was learned then about social influence.

The effect of the presence of others: social facilitation. In 1916, Allport was beginning his doctoral research. His object was to investigate the effect of the presence of others on individual performance. Subjects were asked to perform a variety of tasks including multiplying numbers, crossing out vowels in news articles, free associating, and judging the weight of objects. They performed these tasks under several conditions: while completely alone, while alone but aware that others were working elsewhere at the same time, and while together with others at the same table.

The presence of others had three general effects. First, there was a greater rate of responding on the tasks. For example, people were able to complete more multiplication problems while in the presence of others. Second, however, in the rush and distraction of the others' presence, subjects were less accurate, e.g., they made more mistakes on the arithmetic problems. Third, one had a different orientation in the presence of others—greater concern with what others thought. For instance, free associations were less egocentric and more conversational, and judgments of weight were more moderate. Interestingly, working in isolation, but knowing others were completing the same tasks in other rooms, had the same effect as working in the immediate presence of others.

The heuristic value of Allport's work lies in demonstrating that the mere presence of others can be psychologically important. Also, this research raises two important questions related to social influence (Allport, 1924; Allport, 1962). First, what is it about some collections of people that makes each individual act differently than he would if he were alone? Is it due to some special quality that distinguishes group from individual action? Second, what is it we want to observe and measure when we study collective behavior?

Is collective action something special? Our first question asked if an aggregate of people has a special, superordinate quality. This idea is not new. In the 19th century, the Frenchman Le Bon had maintained that when men joined a crowd, their intelligence was lowered to that of primitive beings (these included the lower classes, women, and children). Later, Gestalt psychologists said that under certain conditions, individual stimuli are perceived as a whole object or pattern. With these data in mind, some became convinced that a collective reality exists above the observable reality of individuals—groups must be more than the sum of individuals in the group.

This notion was attractive because it seemed to "explain" collective phenomena (such as riots and fads). Modern social psychologists, however, reject the idea because it is unscientific, i.e., unobservable and unmeasurable. Further, they refuse to confuse arbitrary concepts with explanations of why events take place—the latter can be tested.

How do we study collective action? Anything we study about collective behavior and belief must be readily translatable into observables, and the only observables at our disposal are the individual actions within aggregates. Everyone uses statements like "that gang likes motorcycles" instead of the more accurate statement "each member of that gang likes motorcycles." But psychologists insist that such summary phrases must be grounded in the actual procedure from which they originated. For example, to say that a certain club is "well-liked" by its members is imprecise unless the statement is based on something observable, such as questionnaires that individual members completed, rankings they made of various clubs, or some other definite procedure.

Defining the Group

Social influence, then, is a change in individuals induced by individuals. Identifying in which aggregates these changes will take place is not simple, however. Remember that Allport obtained what he called "group effects" even when subjects could not see or hear each other. Today, most social psychologists are in basic agreement (cf. Cartwright and Zander, 1968): social influence occurs only in aggregates where the members have some psychological involvement with each other. Now we may ask, where will this involvement be found?

Statistical collections. Statistical collections are aggregates to which people are assigned on the basis of some similarity among them (say, all persons living in the third house on their block). To the extent that this similarity is unknown or unimportant to those within the category, the aggregate is not a group. Psychological involvement with others cannot exist unless one is aware of them.

Kurt Lewin (1948), one of the most influential of early social psychologists, made the following point: "Similarity between persons merely permits their classification, their subsumption under the same abstract concept, whereas belonging to the same social group means concrete, dynamic interrelations among persons. A husband, a wife and a baby are less similar to each other, in spite of their being a strong natural group, than the baby is to other babies . . ." (p. 134).

However, that people are aware of each other is not enough to make them a group. Some statistical collections, based on demographic similarity among persons, are widely known (e.g., Yankees, Republicans, the middle class). Yet for some who supposedly fall into these categories, there is no group. These people are not involved with others in the same aggregate because they do not define themselves as members of it. Take, for example, the "middle class." Assignment to this class is often made on the basis of educational level, financial status, or profession. But many people with the required attributes do not define themselves as middle class. Centers (1949) showed that many such individuals placed themselves in the working class, and others (e.g., Douvan, 1956) have found that it is the class to which one feels he belongs that determines many of his beliefs and actions. In fact, some data in the famous Kinsey report (1948) suggest that one's sexual behavior conforms to that social class to which one aspires, whether one belongs to that class or not.

Membership and reference groups. Being aware of others in the same aggregate and defining oneself as a member may still not guarantee that the individual is involved. Everyone knows people who, although nominally members of a group, nevertheless seem completely uninterested in the group. For them to be real members of a group, they would have to feel kinship or identify with the others—to feel they were significant. Social psychologists would say that these people belong to a *membership group*, since they belong to the group in name only. A psychological group—called a *reference group*—is defined only when (1) the person is aware of the others, (2) the person defines himself as a member, or would like to be a member, and (3) the person feels that the others are significant to him (emotionally or cognitively). Only in such aggregates will psychological involvement be found.

In everyday life, membership and reference groups are not entirely independent. Often one's membership group is, or becomes, a reference group and it is sometimes difficult for a researcher to tell the difference. A well-known study by Siegel and Siegel (1957) illustrates the interaction of the two. In this study, the Siegels administered a personality test, the Ethnocentrism-Fascism (E-F) Scale, to a group of students at Stanford University. The E-F Scale measures conservative attitudes towards society, including one's concern with status. They found that girls who wanted to live in the prestigious Row houses (former sorority houses) tended to score high on the Scale. The Siegels then chose a sample of twenty-eight girls living in the freshman dormitory who wanted to move into Row houses for their sophomore year. Drawings were held each year for living quarters. Of the Siegels' subjects, nine were able to move into a Row house. The others could draw again at the end of their sophomore year, but by this time, only eleven of the remaining nineteen still wanted to move into a Row house.

Thus, at this point three distinct groups had evolved: Nine subjects made up a membership and reference group of Row house occupants. Eleven subjects belonged to a Row house reference group (but not a membership group since they never lived there). Eight subjects belonged to neither a Row house membership nor reference group. To measure the effect of living arrangement and choice on attitudes, the Siegels again administered the E-F Scale. They found that the scores of those living in a Row house had changed hardly at all—they were still highly status oriented. The scores of those not living in, but wanting to live in, a Row house were also altered only slightly. But those who no longer cared about moving into a Row house had changed a great deal. These eight girls scored much lower on the E-F Scale. Only those girls for whom the Row house was a reference group were able to keep their status-oriented attitudes intact. The Siegel study illustrates the role that psychological involvement plays in the impact of the group on the individual.

INDIVIDUAL INVOLVEMENT IN GROUPS

The Formation of Groups

Some reference groups are created for easily discernible reasons (study groups, baseball teams). The reason for the formation of other reference groups is not so clear. Why, for example, do experimental subjects form reference groups? (Luckily for researchers, such groups often emerge in the laboratory.) After all, in many group experiments the subjects are complete strangers, have little in common, and will never see each other again. We believe the answer lies in two general human tendencies. One is that if people perceive some similarity with others (including similarity of attitude, similarity of purpose, common predicament, or sometimes even mere proximity), then they will tend to align themselves with those others. Second, people will establish some structural relation with their fellows, ". . . to be 'not left adrift' but included as a part of a present collectivity; or to help create, if necessary, such a structural relationship so that one *can* be a part of it" (Allport, 1962, p. 14). Allport argues that the tendency to form groups is reinforced by the heightened satisfactions one receives as part of groups (e.g., emotional security).

These notions, however, do not explain why some groups are formed and not others. The conditions causing a person to join a particular group depend also on the functions that the group can serve for him, the "potential satisfactions" to which Allport refers.

The Functions of Reference Groups

Reference groups vary according to their members' motives for joining them and maintaining their place in them. People *use* groups—they get something from them. Kelley (1952) has noted that the uses to which an individual puts a group fall into two general categories. First, he may be motivated to gain or maintain acceptance. Seeking companionship, finding a mate, and showing off fall into this category. Kelley explains that in this case the group is in a position to award or withhold recognition to the person. To the degree that he conforms to the rules and standards of the group he may be rewarded. This type of group has a *normative* function in that it encourages and enforces the enactment of acceptable behavior and belief. In a group having this function, the person will be concerned with who likes whom, with avoiding rejection by the others, and with possible surveillance of his behavior.

One can also use the reference group to increase one's knowledge of the world, or to facilitate evaluations of oneself and others. For instance, in joining a writers' conference, the aspiring writer is using the group to evaluate and perfect his own ability. In this kind of group, the others are merely a standard which the person uses in making judgments about the world, others, or himself. It has an *informational* function. In such a group the person will be concerned with the information he gathers from the group, to see if it is clear or ambiguous, if it is discrepant with his own cognitions, and if it is defined as he defines it.

Of course, a group can, and often does, serve both normative and informational functions. Morton Deutsch and Harold Gerard (1955) conducted a study to investigate the two functions of groups simultaneously. With respect to normative influence, two of their hypotheses were: (1) normative social influence will be greater, the more involved individuals are in a group, and (2) normative social influence will increase when the individual perceives that his actions can be identified with him. Deutsch and Gerard employed Asch's experimental situation to test these hypotheses. In one experimental condition, as in standard Asch studies, the subjects judged lines while face to face with three confederates. In another condition, subjects were separated by partitions and indicated their judgments anonymously by pressing a button. By comparing the differences in conformity between these two groups, the effect of being identifiable could be tested. In a third condition Deutsch and Gerard tried to create an explicit reference group by forcing subjects to be involved with one another. These subjects were treated exactly like those in the anonymous condition but were also told that the most successful group would win tickets to a Broadway play. By comparing this condition to the anonymous condition the effect of an involving group could be tested.

Deutsch and Gerard found that conformity to the (inaccurate) judgments of others was greater when subjects were working for a prize. Conformity also increased when subjects could be identified with their judgments. Can we definitely conclude that the group was actually serving a normative function for the subjects? Perhaps not, but the type of task suggests that it was. If you remember, the correct judgment in the Asch situation is rather obvious. It is unlikely that subjects were looking to the others for information. More probably, they wanted to be acceptable to the others and not "stand out in the crowd."

To investigate informational influence, Deutsch and Gerard also had their subjects judge lines from memory in a second phase of the experiment. After the lines were displayed, they were withdrawn and three seconds elapsed before the first person gave his judgment. However, with the correct line clearly identifiable and such a brief pause, it is unlikely that subjects needed much information from others. Indeed, judgments made from memory and those made directly were relatively similar.

This study suggests how group function relates to social influence. Assume that a subject is motivated to gain acceptance. Assume further that he changes his judgments to facilitate his acceptance (a disagreeable person might be rejected). Now what happens when the group can win a prize? Deviation may lose the prize and, if so, would certainly lead to rejection—so he is more likely to conform. If the group can identify the deviate (as in a face to face interaction), the pressures for conformity are even greater.

Group Goals

How group goals are perceived affects the formation of groups, involvement in groups, and the success of group pressure. Group goals emerge even in newly formed groups. Take, for instance, a bunch of students brought together for an experiment. Each person is supposed to follow the experimenter's directions, including perhaps the request to "act naturally." But what is the group goal? At first there does not seem to be one, but given some time, one will emerge.

We said earlier that people in a common situation will come to perceive themselves as similar to each other, at least to the extent that they perceive themselves in the "same boat." This, plus the motive to be "at one" with the others, will result in the cognitive and emotional feeling that "we are a group." The members of this group will feel a need to justify their existence as a group. So each one, in his own mind, will create a group goal, or, more precisely, goals for the group. As the members of a group continue to interact, individual goals for the group become more and more uniform. We end up with what we call a group goal. The process by which individual goals become more similar to each other has not been studied much, but it is probable that the change in this attitude occurs as do changes in other attitudes. The members of the group will use others' goals as a kind of measuring stick for their own (later we will discuss this process—called the "frame of reference"). Also, to ensure the continuation of the group, they will attempt to avoid conflict with the others, resulting in a convergence of individual goals. They may even explicitly vote on a group goal after discussing its merits.

There have been many studies designed to test various facets of the group goal phenomenon. Below we list several recurrent findings relevant to the study of conformity:

1. When an individual *accepts* his group's goal, he will be motivated to work within the group for its attainment. In most cases, group success will necessitate conformity to at least some of the rules and standards of the group. In one sense, private acceptance of an important group standard—in particular, the group goal—will lead to acceptance of and compliance with other group standards (White and Lippitt, 1968; Schachter, Ellertson, McBride, and Gregory, 1951).

2. The individual must understand the group goal. A *clear* goal enhances conformity to group standards (Raven and Rietsema, 1957).

3. When group standards are *relevant* to the group goal, there is greater pressure for conformity (Schachter, 1951).

4. To the extent that the group can be *successful* in attaining its goals, the individual will conform (Thomas, 1957).

5. The individual who contributes to the success of the group will be highly valued. Members who have higher *status* in the group will have a greater influence on the others (Lippitt, Polansky, Redl, and Rosen, 1952).

6. When cooperation or *interdependence* will help to reach the group goal, conformity will be greater (Deutsch, 1949; Thomas, 1957).

One can infer from our list the importance of the group goal. A group's goals have an effect on the individual's involvement in the group and also affect what behaviors the group finds important to control. For example, a study by Coch and French (1948) suggests that some factory worker groups have an anti-company goal—to produce as little as they can get away with. When workers are given more say in company work policies, their goal alters to be more consistent with the company's. Subsequent intragroup influence attempts may be directed at greater efficiency, rather than greater laxity.

GROUP PRESSURE

The intragroup influence attempts we mentioned above are subsumed under the concept of group pressure. *Group pressure is a psychological force operating upon a person to fulfill others' expectations of him, including especially those expectations of others relating to the person's "roles" or to behaviors specified or implied by the "norms" of the group to which he belongs.*

What is meant by a "force to fulfill others' expectations"? To demonstrate, let us examine what happens when a group has just been formed. Suppose a crowd of strangers are riding on a subway and there is a power failure, trapping them in the train for several hours. We expect that their common predicament would predispose them to perceive themselves as a group—at least for the time being. The implications of this perceptual change are indeed interesting. Once each person has "joined" the group he will be motivated to help keep the group intact, for example by quieting the most anxious. He will also be motivated to keep his own place within the group, and will thus try to accommodate himself to the others. If he were too disagreeable, or acted too dissimilarly, he might not be accepted by the others. So if the others were acting calmly, he would have to overcome his own panic. On the other hand, if the others were overtly nervous, he could not act too disinterested (they might think him a snob or inhuman). It would all depend on what the others expected of him. The end result of attempting to be accommodating would be changes in behavior in accordance with others' expectations, i.e., conformity. In this example, group pressure takes the form of possible rejection by others or possible disintegration of the group. There are other forms of group pressure. Let us examine several experimental situations to show how group pressure operates in different circumstances.

Suppose we have an experiment (or any situation) where individuals have to perform on some task. Subjects will want to maintain a level of performance which will be acceptable to the others. In the usual situation, where "success" involves good performance, each member wants to measure up. So he tries harder, and works more quickly. The crucial component here is what the person thinks the others expect of him. In some cases these expectations may dictate *decreased* rates of performance. Whyte (1943) observed a gang of boys over a period of time. In one case, a boy who bowled quite well alone did very poorly when with his friends. They had assigned him low status within the gang and expected him to do poorly. The boy's survival as a gang member required a low bowling score.

Other situations will require different tactics for maintaining behavior expected by others. Sherif (1935) created a situation where subjects apparently felt that extreme judgments of stimuli would be unacceptable to others. Groups of subjects were asked to judge the extent of the apparent movement of a point of light in a dark room (called the autokinetic effect). Sherif found that as the subjects continued to speak in turn, extreme judgments became less frequent, and the estimates converged. No such effect was found for subjects working alone (see also Allport, 1924). Sherif has hypothesized that in this type of situation the others' judgments are used as a "frame of reference" for the subject's own judgment. That is, the other judgments define the array of possible judgments for each person. With each subject trying to be accommodating, one should find the most extreme judgments dropping out and more "average" judgments becoming increasingly popular. Group pressure, in this case, induces moderation.

In sum, group pressure is the motivating force behind conformity. As our discussion indicates, there may be a number of reasons why people pay attention to the expectations of others. Assuming initial involvement in the group, the individual may conform to avoid rejection, to ingratiate himself, to be "one of the boys," and so forth. The individual motives which make group pressure so effective are more fully detailed in the next section.

Why Group Pressure Is Effective

The forces acting on members of group to fulfill the other's expectations of them are effective because people pay attention to the others in the group and care about what they think. We have been saying this all along: psychological involvement in a group ensures both the presence and acceptance of group pressure. But as we noted earlier, reference groups serve different functions for the individual. This means that the reason why a particular individual is involved with the group and is attending to others' expectations may vary depending on the use to which he is putting the group. So there are actually many individual motives which act to make group pressure effective. We mentioned them before, but let us review them now.

Motives for attending to group expectations. Individual motives for fulfilling others' expectations fall into two general categories. First, a person may respond to group pressure because the group is serving a normative function for him. He attempts to live up to the expectations of others because:

1. The others will accept and like him, or will not reject him,
2. The group goal will be successfully attained,
3. The continuation of the group will be ensured.

People may also fulfill others' expectations as a by-product of informational, or cognitve, needs. Thus, if the group has an informational function, the others' expectations can serve as a guide for:

1. Gaining "correct"information about reality.
2. Validating one's own opinions and making sure they are consistent with the opinions of others.
3. Evaluating oneself and others.

These individual motives explain why people respond to group pressure. But the effectiveness of the pressure will also depend on how explicit others' expectations are. Therefore, we must discuss the means by which their expectations are transmitted.

How group expectations are transmitted. The expectations of the group are sometimes made very explicit, as when there are written rules for behavior or when group leaders give commands. But expectations need not be overtly transmitted to be perfectly clear. The individual only has to perceive that his beliefs or acts disagree with those of the group. Try to imagine the expectations that are transmitted in the following examples:

> An experimenter read off the questionnaire results: "I see that you thought the orange painting was best. The rest of the group thought the blue and green one was much better."

> A textile worker was commended for turning out 100 pajama tops in one day—while observed by the others in her work group (who turned out only 50).

We are fairly certain that in each example certain expectations are being perceived. Some research on imitation in children (cf. Bandura, 1965) suggests that group expectations are readily understood even if they are not explicit. These studies are relevant to group pressure because (1) the dependent variables were usually the extent to which a child would copy a model acting in a novel manner—called imitation, but analogous to our term compliance, and (2) the independent variables included the presence or absence of explicit suggestions that the subject should change. Although the manipulations were not designed for that purpose, explicitness seemingly was varied through the use of rewards or punishments given to the subject, or the model, for compliance. Briefly, the data indicated that novel responses are noticed and learned through observation of a model, alone, while the actual performance of those responses, compliance itself, is affected by the extent to which the subject (or model) is rewarded for complying. Apparently, we learn early in life to pay attention to others, especially when their behavior differs from ours. However, whether we act on apparent discrepancies between others and ourselves seems to depend partly on whether, through reward or punishment, it becomes clear that others really want us to change.

Assuming, now, that implicit or explicit group pressure is relatively easy to perceive, and that the individual will often be motivated to accept group pressure, what kinds of behavior or belief will change? To predict what will change, we must first know what behaviors or beliefs the group is most interested in controlling. The answer is found in our formal definition of group pressure: "group pressure is a psychological force . . . to fulfill others' expectations . . . *especially those expectations relating to the person's roles or to behaviors specified or implied by the norms of the group . . .*"

Norms and Roles

The group is not interested in all the behavior of its members. It is concerned that members conform to its norms and play the roles assigned to them. Norms and roles refer to certain expectations that are salient to the group because of their relevance to the survival of the group and to the efficiency and pleasantness of group interaction.

Norms. A norm is a standard or rule of conduct and belief specified, implicitly or explicitly, by a group, society, or culture. For example, smiling a great deal is an implicit American norm. What determines which norms will emerge in a group? By now, the student should have some idea because the motives that each individual has for joining and maintaining membership in a group will interact with the others' motives to determine the norms that the group has. The most important norms will be those that hold the group together and smooth interpersonal interaction, since motive satisfaction depends so much on these factors. Some norms become rituals and look silly to outsiders (e.g., secret handclasps). However, these norms can increase members' security, help to define the group, and give the impression of uniqueness.

Below are some examples of the kinds of norms that are likely to emerge in groups:

1. When individuals are committed to each other because of situational factors (e.g., they work together) or because their past interaction has aroused emotional ties, they will want future interaction to be as smooth as possible. Norms requiring "polite" behavior or "moderate" attitudes may become strong. A series of experiments by Kiesler, Kiesler, and Pallak (1967) bear on the relationship of commitment to future interaction to cultural norms. In one of the experiments, subjects were either committed to working with their partners in the future, or would never see them again. Some subjects heard a bogus tape in which their partners insulted the experimenter. The insult involved expressing extremely negative attitudes about secretaries—the experimenter's former occupation. The subjects' reactions to this *faux pas* depended on whether or not they would have to work with their partners in the future. If they were not committed to future interaction, they tended to ignore their partners' behavior. But when they were committed, they openly expressed concern that the partners act "correctly."

2. Sometimes the success of the group goal will depend on the members expressing extreme attitudes and personal feelings, or on the enactment of less "cultured" behaviors. For example, therapy groups must reveal and discuss hidden thoughts and feelings so that, by sharing them, each patient can learn more realistic ways of feeling and acting. In one of the Kiesler, Kiesler, and Pallak experiments there was an analogous situation. Students at Yale University participated in a group "problem-solving" experiment. The atmosphere of the experiment was varied to create different group goals. In one condition, the experimenter formally and carefully presented the experiment as if it were very important to him. In another condition, he was dressed sloppily, and casually introduced the experiment as if it were an extra duty. Throughout the experiment, a confederate acted impolitely and disrespectfully. Another "control" confederate acted normally. Later in the

session, subjects rated the two confederates. The data showed that, compared to the normal confederate, the impolite confederate was disliked. But negative reactions to him were much greater when the atmosphere of the experiment was serious rather than casual. Presumably, the serious dress and demeanor of the experimenter encouraged the group members to be formal and task-oriented; the goal might have been to get the job done or to please the experimenter. Since in that case norms requiring attention to the task, respect for the experimenter, and politeness would be important, it is not surprising that these subjects disliked the confederate who fooled around.

3. The group serving an informational function for its members is often less concerned with manners and the pleasantness of interaction. Instead the group imposes standards that will provide the maximum amount of the desired information, and the least disquieting means of evaluating others and oneself. In discussing some data from the World War II studies of the American soldier, Kelley (1952) noted that combat veterans had "a strong group code against any tendencies to glamorize or express eagerness for combat." We can guess that in the face of danger, unambiguous information on how to behave was essential for survival. Moreover, unrealistic bravado would have contradicted the evidence of the senses. Of course, the green troops were also insecure and in need of information. But without the evidence of combat, optimistic evaluations of the situation would be the most comfortable and self-enhancing kinds of information to have. Hence, the emergence of "blood and thunder" norms would reduce anxiety while increasing "manliness" and patriotism—that is, until war became a reality.

Roles. Many norms govern a set of expectations about how the typical occupant of a given position in a group is supposed to behave. There is the role of college teacher, a role of United States President, and a role of husband. Regardless of who occupies these positions, people will tend to expect certain behaviors of those in the role. For example, a "wife" is expected to defer to her husband, make sure the house is well kept, and so forth. Some research has been done with respect to what roles will emerge in a particular group. For example, the member who is most successful at attaining the group goal will be expected to play the role of "leader." Thus, the person's expected role will, at least to some extent, be determined by the actual function he has in the group. In addition, the power an individual has over the others in a group will partly determine the role he is expected to play. Finally, the situation itself will determine what roles are expected. If the group must cooperate to succeed, the members will be expected to play the role of "partner." If they must compete, they will be expected to play the role of "combatant."

It should be apparent by now that norms and roles prescribe a great deal of our everyday lives. With group pressure to make sure we conform to those norms and roles, much of our lives would seem to be routine and predictable. But obviously this is not true. One of several reasons is that the norms of the various groups we belong to may conflict.

Conflicting Group Expectations

When different groups with which the individual is associated have discrepant values and attitudes, they will also have different expectations for the individual. He will, therefore, be in conflict. To which group should he conform? Not everyone encounters such a situation, however. The reason is that a person's many reference groups are likely to be similar in most respects. Usually, a person would not join both the American Civil Liberties Union and the Ku Klux Klan.

But conflicts sometimes occur. One's reaction to such a situation depends on a number of factors. Certainly, the group that the individual is with, or is thinking about, at the time of the conflict will have an advantage. The student who is reminded that she is Catholic will have more pro-Church attitudes than one who is not (cf. Charters and Newcomb, 1958). Another relatively obvious factor is how important each group is to the individual. The more a person identifies with a group, the greater its relative influence. Converse and Campbell (1968) once conducted an extensive study of voting behavior which illustrates the relationship between group identification and conformity. They interviewed over 1500 members of unions, church groups, and minorities. One finding was that people who felt their group was important to them were more likely to vote "with the group" than were more indifferent members. One very influential group was the trade union. When some unions came out strongly for the Democratic candidate for president in 1956, 81% of those who strongly identified with the union voted for that candidate. Of those who identified less strongly, only 50% voted for the candidate.

Role conflict. Most of us occupy a number of roles in our social life, often more than one at any given time. In analyzing the effect of a particular group on an individual, we must be careful to inspect whether the person's role conflicts with his role in another group. The ability of people to keep their social roles disparate has become almost a cliché. For example, witness the businessman who behaves ruthlessly during the week and faithfully attends church on Sunday. Nonetheless there are conditions under which these roles do come into conflict. Gross, McEachern, and Mason (1958) have noted the conflicting role demands made upon school superintendents. They found that the school superintendent has three roles to play: the role of school superintendent from the point of view of the school board; the role of school superintendent as regarded by the parents; and his role vis-a-vis the teachers within the school system. The school board wants the school run smoothly and as inexpensively as possible. The parents would like to see their children in smaller classes, but not at the expense of a tax increase. The teachers want higher salaries. At particular times of the year these three roles become especially divergent, and the conflict thus produced for the school superintendent becomes torturous indeed. It should be apparent that the extent to which norms or roles conflict may affect how one behaves in a group, and specifically how one reacts to the group's influence attempts.

Social psychologists have attempted to sort through the various factors contributing to the acceptance or rejection of group standards by studying the total situation confronting a person when he interacts with others. It is especially important to consider how the group member perceives the situation he is in. Group pressure will affect these perceptions and in doing so will indirectly influence the form and extent of conformity.

Some Other Effects of Group Pressure on the Individual

Group pressure leads a person to view the world in certain ways. For example, the group defines what is "correct" social behavior. It has been found that what is perceived as correct in a group situation may actually be more "risky" or more reckless than is ordinarily true for individuals. Individuals tend to take more chances as group members (e.g., Kogan and Wallach, 1967), and they also may act less politely (Singer, Brush and Lublin, 1965). Festinger, Pepitone, and Newcomb (1952) called the tendency for group members to become less "civilized," *deindividuation,* because they thought that individuals feel less identifiable (i.e., less likely to have to take personal blame) when in groups.

Deindividuation has been attributed to the reduced fear of negative consequences for an individual if he acts within the group. This notion has broad implications for behavior in riots, mobs, and panic situations. However, the hypothesis does not account for the obvious increase in constraint that occurs in some groups (hence the term "company manners"). Perhaps the presence or absence of constraint depends on the cultural norms most salient in the particular situation. Brown (1965) suggests that risk-taking in experimental groups may increase because the subjects do not want to appear cowardly when they think the group values risk. Perhaps if these same subjects were actual executives at a staff meeting they would value conservatism more. Unfortunately, there is little experimental research on which to base predictions about which cultural norms will be salient in a given situation.

The group defines not only what is "correct," but many other factors in the situation. It may, for example, define whether the situation is dangerous or not. Cantril (1958) documented a panic which occurred in 1938 due to a radio broadcast by Orson Welles. A number of people thought the broadcast was a newscast describing an invasion by Martians, when it actually was a play. One factor determining whether or not a person panicked was the attitudes of those around him. If he looked out the window and saw people calmly strolling around, he "realized" the news flash was a fake. If he saw someone running to a car, he prepared to run from the Martians too.

The group can also define a person's own place in society at large. In 1954, the Supreme Court heard how Afro-American children learn from other Afro-Americans that their skin color makes them inferior (see Clark and Clark, 1958). In the Clarks' study, these children chose white dolls to play with and rejected brown dolls. Conversely, belonging to a particular group can also define one as "superior." In fact, this is the major function of some groups (e.g., The Society of Those Who Came Over on the *Mayflower*).

Summary

As can be seen from our discussion, the group has a powerful impact on the individual. The group affects one's perceptions of the world and of oneself, induces modifications in beliefs and opinions, and causes changes in behavior. We defined alterations toward the expectations of the group as conformity. The psychological force—group pressure—causing one to conform is a complex of individual motives and group expectations. In short, a group member cares about the group and is involved with the others in the group. That he attends to their expectations and tries to act as they wish follows from his involvement. That they have certain expectations for each other follows from their involvement. The mutual attempt to be accommodating, to keep the group intact, and to maintain acceptability results in conformity.

This chapter on group pressure did not deal in detail with the crucial "why" questions in the study of conformity. That is, under what conditions will conformity—compliance or private acceptance—take place? The last three chapters will take up this question. Chapter 3 will discuss compliance. Chapters 4 and 5 will discuss private acceptance. These chapters will describe the research which has been undertaken and the major issues confronting the researcher in conformity.

CHAPTER THREE

Compliance

In all research on compliance, the emphasis is on behavior—does the person *do* what another person or group "wants" him to? The beliefs and attitudes of the person are either left untested (as in early research) or de-emphasized (as in the more modern approach). The current concern is how we get people to do something or not to do something; their beliefs and attitudes are of secondary or no interest.

We do not wish to underestimate the problem of compliance. Indeed, many would insist that from the practical point of view, the study of compliance is more important than that of private acceptance. For example, one problem facing this country is the employment of handicapped people. We know that employers are unduly reticent about hiring the handicapped, or at least various kinds of them for particular jobs. Handicapped people are indeed handicapped, of course, but the hiring ratio is much lower than reality would demand. Consequently, a major task is to increase the frequency of that behavior—hiring the handicapped. An additional problem is that the handicapped, partly as a result of discouraging experiences, are cautious about applying for a job. So there are really two questions here: not only, "How do we induce employers to hire the handicapped when they apply?", but also, "How do we induce the handicapped to apply for jobs in the first place?" For people involved in this critical area, attitude change or private acceptance is really of secondary importance. They are interested in behavior change and are willing to worry about attitude change later, if at all. Inducing people to vote in elections, to contribute to worthy causes, to behave "tolerantly" toward minority groups, and to take active roles in community affairs are similar problems in that behavior change is the critical issue.

Practical issues pervade our lives. For example, until recently, Yale College had no women students and the undergraduates' dates had to be imported from Smith, Vassar, Connecticut College, and the like for weekend visits. If it were sex the Yale man wanted, he had only the weekend. Strategies of compliance had to be quickly implemented. As one undergraduate put it, "It's a practical problem in social psychology: the study of compliance—and private acceptance be damned!"

But, as Kurt Lewin once said, there is nothing so practical as a good theory. Unfortunately, early research on conformity was not very theoretically oriented, and there was seldom even an attempt to distinguish between compliance and private acceptance. This early research was quite simple by modern standards, and not attuned to the psychological process behind conformity. The questions of why a particular effect occurred, when it would occur, and when it would not, were seldom asked. As we have suggested, in the process of continually asking why subjects in a given condition conform, we become more precise and more theoretical. It is our explanation—our theory—that allows us to generalize to other situations. Before we can say if conformity will occur in a second situation, we need to answer the question of why it occurred in the first situation. (See Kiesler, 1969).

The early research was quite atheoretical, but considering its practical and historical importance, it demands discussion. To begin, issues of general concern in the study of compliance will be reviewed. We will then examine the older experimental models for studying compliance and follow this with some of the research they stimulated. Later in the chapter, more recent work will be reviewed, particularly that emphasizing theory.

WHY COMPLY?

Several topics of general concern are explored below. One will recognize the relationship of the discussion to Allport's basic *raison d'etre* of groups—to be at one with others—but none of the issues has received much experimental attention. For example, the need to be liked has not been directly manipulated in experimental research. Contemplation of these issues, however, provides one with a good introduction to compliance and illustrates the importance of controlling certain variables in experimental research.

Group Goal

As mentioned in Chapter 2, it is often necessary that a group, formal or informal, "put on a united front" in order to succeed. For the group to be perceived as accomplishing something, it often must also be perceived as not having internal disagreement. For example, one never hears the President announce, "After much wrangling and argument in my council of advisors, resulting in still considerable disagreement, I have decided . . . ." Similarly, in contract negotiations with unions, the company negotiator always talks about the "company's position," even though there may be considerable disagreement among the higher echelon in the company about what the company's position is.

Of course, there is nothing wrong with a particular group presenting a united front publicly. Often the united front is necessary for the group to accomplish its goal. Whether the group is a family or a departmental faculty, dissenters may be expected to "go along with" the group, whether they agree privately or not. Sometimes there is an implicit social exchange involved in such public compliance without private acceptance. This is, it is implicitly assumed that if I go along with you this time, then at some time in the future you will have to go along with me. I will accept your tactic for accomplishing one subgoal of our group if you will accept my tactic for accomplishing another subgoal. Sometimes in larger groups, such as state and national legislatures or bureaucracies, subgoals are subjected to so much bargaining that the resulting group goal is a mish-mash of conflicting and possibly competing subgoals. An amendment, tacked onto a bill to appease a small group of legislators, may be irrelevant or even take all the verve and dash out of the bill's intent.

A spirit of public accommodation allows the group to continue its progress towards ultimate goals. For example, consider the following experimental paradigm actually used several times. A subject is told that his group will win a prize only if their opinion is unanimous on some issue or judgment, and if it is correct. The subject then finds that the group (actually a bunch of confederates) has a unanimous opinion but one which he thinks is incorrect. What will he do? If he can't change the others, he will make his judgment or opinion identical to that of the group. Since the group judgment must be unanimous to win the prize, it is the only chance the subject has to win. In this particular case, one does not even have to talk about group goals. If the individual's goal is to win, then he has only one strategy to use. Mutual accommodation has often been mistaken for private acceptance, however, as the next chapter will detail.

The Need to Be Liked

People like others who have attitudes similar to theirs and who behave like them (cf. Byrne, 1961). When people are asked to ingratiate themselves with another person, i.e., try to get the other person to like them, one of the techniques they use is to voice opinions similar to those of the other, to agree with the other. In experiments on compliance, more attractive or high-status group members induce proportionally high compliance on the part of the subject. We apparently think that if we act somewhat like others, they will like us more. Some research on ingratiation suggests that people implicitly assume this to be true, even though they may not be able to describe their feeling explicitly. The need to be liked seems to be a very powerful variable. For example, Berenda (1950) has found that children are more likely to conform to the judgments or opinions of their peers than they are to those of their teachers. Apparently, the higher status held by the teachers is not strong enough to overcome the need to be liked by one's peers.

Of course, it is not that we conform just to be liked more. It is often that we conform to avoid being rejected. For example, consider the Schachter (1951) experiment mentioned in Chapter 2. Schachter used three confederates in each group. The difference among these confederates was the opinions they expressed during the group's interaction. One of the confederates, called the "mode," tried always to express opinions which were approximately those being expressed by the naive members of the group. Another confederate, called the "slider," initially expressed opinions quite different from the naive members', but later in the group interaction gradually moved his public opinions towards those being voiced by the group. A third confederate, most important for our point here, was called the "deviate." He continued to hold deviant opinions. Schachter was interested in two dependent measures: the patterns of communication to the three stooges and their acceptance by the group members. As the experimental hour progressed, more and more communication was directed towards the deviate. However, towards the end of the experimental hour, this communication dropped off, suggesting that the group had first tried to induce the deviate to change his opinion, and when this failed, decided to ignore him. Various measures of the attractiveness of the deviate bore this out. The group found the deviate less attractive than either the slider or the mode, suggesting that they had indeed rejected him. Thus, the consequences of deviation within a group appear quite clear. First, one can expect a great deal of pressure put upon the deviate to change his opinions towards the greater accord of the group. If this fails, one can expect rejection.

The Maintenance of Existing Relationships

This section cannot be clearly divorced from "the need to be liked." Nonetheless, there are some data that one feels a little uncomfortable about explaining with reference to a need to be liked. In a number of circumstances it is necessary to adopt particular behaviors because of the views of others, even when these behaviors mean little to us. Acquiescence is helped along by the need to be liked by another, the liking for another, empathy for another's situation, and just the necessity of continuing the relationship. For example, many accommodations are made between roommates in a college dormitory about studying habits, time to go to bed, picking up clothes, and so forth. It does not seem correct to say that one changes one's behavior to accommodate the other simply because one wants to be liked by the other—indeed there are often hostile undercurrents to such relationships. There is a kind of trading off, maximizing reward and minimizing punishment, if you will, that is necessary for the individuals in this pair to continue living with minimum fuss. Compliant behavior that is not directly related to the need to be liked also occurs in families. Children conform overtly, sometimes, to the wishes of their parents (and vice versa) simply because there is a sympathy or understanding of the attitudes or position of the other. If the behavior in question is simply very unimportant to the first actor, he complies with the wishes of the other without feeling a great deal of emotional involvement or loss as a result.

The Need to Be Correct

People apparently develop a strong need to be personally and socially "correct" in their behavior and opinions. Of course, for any given society, what is correct is not always explicitly defined for every situation. However, one easy definition of correctness is the behavior of relevant others. Naturally others do not always provide us with valid cues for being correct. There is a very old story about a visitor for tea at the White House. He was very nervous and not quite sure how to behave. When the tea was served, the visitor was anxiously watching the President to see how he would behave. The President poured milk in his tea; the visitor poured milk in his tea. The President put sugar in his tea; the visitor put sugar in his tea. The President poured some of his tea into his saucer. The visitor was perplexed but anxious not to appear out of place. He poured tea in his saucer. Then the President put his saucer on the floor for his dog.

If we are not certain how to behave or what to believe in a particular situation, we attend to the behavior of others. This principle provides the basis for what has been called social comparison theory, initially proposed by Leon Festinger (1954). Festinger proposes that there are two types of "reality" for a person. One type is called *physical reality*. In physical reality, there are right or wrong, yes or no answers to questions. One example Festinger uses is the question of whether a given material is breakable or not. If we really want to know, we can test it with a hammer. (The question could only be asked once.) However, much of our environment is not so clearly defined: there are often no right or wrong, yes or no answers to questions that are posed. In this type of situation, called social reality, Festinger proposes that individuals will look to others for answers or definitions of the situation, particularly regarding the "correctness" of opinions.

But social comparison is usually done with reference to people not very dissimilar to ourselves. Probably we would compare ourselves to a relevant neighbor or peer more than to the U.S. Chief Protocol Officer when questioning the correctness of our social behavior. In addition to opinions, the theory proposes that we compare ourselves to relevant and similar others regarding abilities. A mathematics major asking himself the question, "Am I any good at mathematics?" will compare himself with other mathematics majors at his university rather than to Albert Einstein. Moreover, he should compare himself to his friends rather than to the total group of mathematics majors.

Social comparison theory suggests several interesting things about compliance. First of all, since we compare ourselves with people not very discrepant from our own opinions or abilities, we tend to come off rather well in the comparison. Unfavorable comparison becomes relatively unlikely, and the judgmental or behavioral system becomes more stable. The theory also suggests that if we are quite discrepant from others in our judgments or behavior (as was the deviate in Schachter's experiment), we will attempt to redefine the situation so that this unfavorable comparison is no longer made. That is, we will redefine the relevance of the others who maintain the different opinions or behaviors. We should try to escape from such a group, seek out new friends, peers, or colleagues with whom a less odious comparison could be made.

EARLY EXPERIMENTAL TECHNIQUES

The Sherif Technique

Sherif was one of the first people to do experimental research on conformity, apparently beginning in the early 1930's. We have previously mentioned his work with regard to the development of norms. To review, Sherif's technique takes advantage of a peculiar but well-known perceptual effect, commonly called the autokinetic phenomenon. If a person sits in a darkened room and is shown a small spot of light, the light appears to move or waver. Hence the name autokinetic, meaning essentially self-moving. The perception of movement appears to be very reliable and occurs for almost everyone. In the norm formation studies, the judgments of naive subjects are allowed to develop without interference. In conformity studies, a confederate or group of confederates gives judgments discrepant from those of the subject. The dependant variable is the degree to which the subject changes his estimate of the light's movement to fit that of the group more closely.

If a person is alone while making his judgments, he will develop a stable frame of reference very quickly. That is, all of his judgments of the light's movement will be within a relatively small range. Let us say that the person perceives the light to move about four inches on the average. If we now place him with a confederate and have them alternate making judgments, the situation will change. If the confederate judges the light to move approximately ten inches on the average, then the subject will gradually increase his judgment of the movement.

This judgmental change is very reliable and has been used in many experiments on conformity. Many writers in the field view these studies as dealing with compliance reactions, but Sherif disagrees. Sherif has argued, quite effectively we think, that this cannot be called compliance.

Sherif describes his situation as one in which there is total ambiguity. The subject perceives that the light wavers but really has no idea how far it moves. Sherif argues that the subject has no frame of reference in which to make a judgment, but he tries his best. As a result of making tentative guesses, the subject develops a frame of reference within which subsequent judgments are made. The confederate then disrupts this frame of reference and at least implicitly provides a new one. After hearing a confederate's discrepant judgments, the subject will typically increase his own estimate to match the confederate's more closely, but he does not think that the light's movement has changed. That is, the subject who formerly judged the light to move an average of four inches and now judges it to move an average of about ten inches still thinks that the light is moving about the same amount. He just feels that he formerly made inaccurate appraisals of the number of inches equivalent to the distance moved. In a sense, it is the scale of judgment that has changed rather than one's perceptions.

Sherif's work can best be viewed as related to the process by which a person develops a frame of reference in a totally ambiguous situation. Actually there is quite a bit of evidence supporting such a view of Sherif's work. For example, the changed frame of reference that the subject develops in response to the confederate's judgments is very stable. If the subject returns the next day to make private judgments, the influence of the confederate is still apparent. Indeed, some (e.g., Rohrer, Baron, Hoffman, and Swander, 1954) have even found this changed frame of reference to persist for as long as a year. In an interesting experiment, Jacobs and Campbell (1961) also investigated the persistence of change with the Sherif technique.

Jacobs and Campbell employed a four-man group, but three of the four men were confederates. The confederates voiced judgments discrepant from the subject's and, as usual, the dependent variable was how much the subject changed his judgments to be more like the confederates'. However, Jacobs and Campbell went one step further. After a series of trials, they removed one of the confederates from the situation and added another naive subject to the group of four. The trials then went on. Later, another one of the confederates was removed and a third naive subject added to the group. Still later, the last confederate was removed and a fourth naive subject was added. The long series of trials began with three confederates and one naive subject and ended with four naive subjects. Jacobs and Campbell did not doubt that the three confederates would have a substantial impact on the one naive subject. However, they were interested in whether this changed frame of reference would be "transmitted" to each

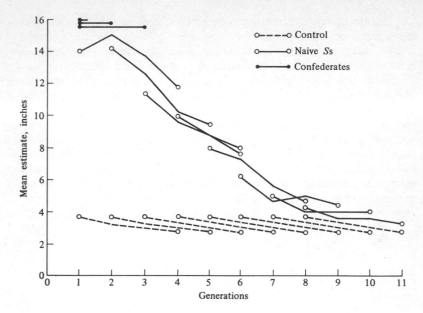

Fig. 3-1. Transmission of an arbitrary norm in four-person groups, when confederates are gradually removed. A "generation" is a block of 30 trials in an autokinetic setting, after which a confederate (if any are left) or the most experienced subject is removed and replaced by a naive subject. (From Jacobs and Campbell, 1961, p. 653.)

ensuing group, particularly when there were no confederates left in the group. Figure 3-1 presents these data.

We can see from Figure 3-1 that the control subjects (with no confederates present) said that the light moved approximately four inches. In the experimental group, the confederates said that it moved 16 inches on the average. In what Jacobs and Campbell call the "first generation," we can see that the confederates had a dramatic impact on the one naive subject in each group. These subjects made estimates of approximately 14 inches. In generation 2 one of the confederates had left and another naive subject had taken his place. The effect of the initial norm was still clear. In generation 3 there was only one confederate left but the naive subjects still made judgments in excess of 12 inches. In generation 4, all confederates had left, and the group consisted of four naive subjects, some more experienced than others. Nonetheless, their judgments of the movement of the light were highly different from those of the controls. In generations 5, 6, and 7 the most experienced subject was removed and another naive subject placed into the group. The effect still persisted at generation 7, even though all of the original group had long since departed. Of course, as we can see, the effect gets smaller and smaller.

The ambiguity of the Sherif setting leaves the subject bereft of any idea of what the correct answer is. The subject "knows" the light moved, but he is very uncertain how far it moved, and anyone's guess is as good or better than his. Perhaps we cannot call such systematic changes in estimates of movement compliance. Given traditional views of compliance as behavior change without private acceptance, this paradigm probably has little to do with compliance, unless the discrepancy between the judgments of the subject and confederate is huge. With a large discrepancy the subject might be confident the group is wrong, or, that whatever the correct judgment is, the group's estimate is much too large. A huge discrepancy is the central component in the discussion to follow of the Asch paradigm.

The Asch Technique

We discussed the Asch technique earlier, but recall that the stimulus situation is almost the opposite of that of Sherif. Whereas Sherif's subject faces an extremely ambiguous stimulus, there is no uncertainty for Asch's subjects. Asch also employs a group of people, all but one of whom are confederates. The group is presented with judgments to make and they make them sequentially, usually the confederates first. On a given trial, the group ordinarily sees two or three lines and they merely say which one matches a comparison line. On most trials, the confederates give the correct answer. However, on some trials interjected throughout the series, the confederates give an incorrect answer. The dependent variable is whether the subject will go along (or comply) with this judgment. Usually, the correct answer is obvious and the subject is certain that the group is wrong. Asch's technique clearly tests for compliance without private acceptance, and he finds that approximately a third of the subjects comply.

Asch's early work concentrated on such variables as the size and composition of the group, the ambiguity of the stimulus, and certain aspects of the conformers' personality. He has found, for example, that three confederates will produce just as much compliance as any larger number. That is, he found that two confederates produce more compliance than one confederate, and three produce more than two, but there is little gained by increasing the number of confederates beyond three. Asch also found that the confederates' judgments must be unanimous to produce compliance. If even one of the confederates gives the correct answer there is almost no compliance on the part of the subject. (See also Asch, 1952, 1958, for other experimental variations.)

The reader is probably already familiar with these early Asch experiments and there is no need to go into them in more detail. We need only add that the technique necessitates the use of several confederates for each subject. This is not only a little clumsy but it is also very expensive. Consequently a technique devised by Crutchfield has become popular.

The Crutchfield Technique

The Crutchfield technique is designed so that several subjects can participate at the same time. "Five subjects at a time are seated side by side in individual booths, screened from one another. Each booth has a panel with a row of numbered switches which the person uses to signal his judgments on items presented on slides projected on the wall in front of the group. Also displayed on his panel are signal lights which indicate what judgments the other four members are giving the items. The booths are designated by letters a, b, c, d, and e, and the subjects are instructed to respond one at a time, in that order." (Krech, Crutchfield, and Ballachey, 1962, p. 509.) Each subject can see the stimulus items (lines or whatever) presented by a slide projector on a screen in front of all the subjects. On a given item he can also see what the others' judgments are by the lights in front of him. Actually, however, everything is controlled by the experimenter. Each subject thinks that he is subject e. As a result, bogus judgments from "subjects" a, b, c, and d can be fed electronically by the experimenter to each of the booths at the same time. Providing the subject believes all this, Crutchfield's technique has several obvious advantages over that of the Asch technique: five subjects, more or less, can be run at the same time, one does not have to pay confederates, and one does not have to worry about the acting ability of the confederates.

Because of their early invention and continued use, the paradigms of Sherif, Asch, and Crutchfield all deserve to be called the classic paradigms in the study of compliance, with the Sherif technique less clearly meeting the requirements of a compliance method. The basic aspects of the methodological techniques for studying compliance without private acceptance often are: a rather obvious and clear-cut judgment perceived by the subject; the group then makes a very discrepant and incorrect judgment; and last, the subject is asked to give his opinion or judgment. The dependent variable is always the change in the subject's judgment towards that "advocated" by the group.

USE OF THE CLASSICAL TECHNIQUES

A Decisional Analysis

Harold Gerard (1965) has given us a very cogent analysis of the subject's state in the compliance conflict. He emphasizes the decision implicit in the Asch situation. According to Gerard, the subject is faced with two choice alternatives. He may either comply with the group's judgment or he may remain independent. Each of these alternatives has negative characteristics associated with it. If the subject complies, then he is not standing out from the crowd or disagreeing with the group or perhaps making himself look silly; but on the other hand, he is publicly making a statement that is quite contrary to his physical senses. This should produce a state of dissonance in the subject (Festinger, 1964).

For the present discussion, dissonance can be regarded as bits of information about the world and oneself that do not fit together. Dissonance should be produced by the knowledge that "I know line A is longer than line B" and the knowledge that "I publicly stated that line B was the longer line." Dissonance is theoretically uncomfortable and the subject should be motivated to reduce it, perhaps by changing his behavior or his opinions or distorting his view of the world. In this example, dissonance could be reduced by the subject convincing himself that the group is a marvelous one and he did the whole thing for them. (See Chapter 5 for a more complete discussion of dissonance theory; see also Zimbardo and Ebbesen, in this series.)

The subject who decides to remain independent is also in an uncomfortable state. The independent subject is indeed behaving according to his physical senses, but now he is publicly disagreeing with the unanimous judgment of his peers, thereby facing possible ridicule or embarrassment. In each case, Gerard says, the subject should be in a state of dissonance, and as a result of this dissonance, he will attempt to justify his decision, perhaps by distorting his evaluation of the group. Having justified his decision, the subject should remain consistent throughout the experimental session. If he complies on the first trial, then he should consistently comply with the group for the rest of the hour. If he elects to remain independent on the first trial, then he should remain independent on the subsequent trials.

This theoretical analysis led Gerard to inspect the Asch paradigm more closely. He reasoned that the decision whether to comply or not is really only present on the first trial. Further, he reasoned that the decision is clear only if there are just two choice alternatives. This led him to predict that in an Asch situation when there are only two choice alternatives, i.e., two comparison lines, one should obtain this consistency of response over trials. On the other hand, when there are three alternatives (three comparison lines) a different situation prevails. On bogus trials in the three-alternative case, the group always chooses the line most discrepant from the correct one. The presence of a line of intermediate length allows a subject to make a compromise between his judgment and that of the group. This compromise judgment in a sense allows a subject to avoid deciding whether to comply or not. If he elects the compromise judgment, he neither completely goes along with the group nor does he completely stick to his own perceptions. He can continue to give the compromise judgment, or he can decide whether he wants to comply or not later in the series. The compromise allows him to defer this decision, in Gerard's view. Therefore, where three alternatives are possible, we should observe much more variation in subjects' behavior from trial to trial. When only two alternatives are possible, each subject should decide whether to comply or not and stick to it.

Gerard's data dramatically fit his hypothesis. When subjects were given a choice between two comparison lines, their overall compliance scores were bimodal over a series of trials. This bimodality means that, in a frequency distribution of number of times that a subject conforms, subjects either comply very often or very seldom. This is precisely what Gerard would expect from his decisional analysis. On the other hand, when subjects were presented with three comparison lines, a more normal distribution was obtained.

Gerard's analogy of the typical compliance experiment as a decision forced upon the subject can be generalized to a number of other experiments using the classical paradigms. When the subject is clearly faced with a choice of whether to comply or not, as in the two-comparison-line case, he is in a state of conflict. He must decide which to do. A number of situational variables, like self-confidence or the status of the group or the ambiguity of the stimulus, could lead him to decide one way or the other. Any one of these might presumably be enough to tip him in a given direction. However, once having decided, a subject is committed to his decision and theoretically feels the need to justify it by remaining consistently a complier or noncomplier in subsequent trials. The subject is psychologically "stuck" with whichever behavior he chooses.

This notion of being committed to a particular behavior in a compliance situation is reminiscent of an experiment by Deutsch and Gerard (1955) that we discussed earlier. Recall that they had two types of variation in their experiment. In one variation they manipulated whether the subject had to make his judgment in an Asch situation publicly before the group or could make it anonymously. Of course, when the subject had to state his opinion or judgment publicly before the rest of the group, he complied with their judgment much more than if he could make that judgment privately. In another variation, Deutsch and Gerard manipulated the degree to which the subject was committed to his initial opinion before he heard the confederates' judgments. In one condition, there was no prior commitment at all. In another condition, subjects wrote their judgments down on a magic pad prior to hearing the judgments made by the others. After each trial they could merely lift the top of the pad and erase the judgment. In a third variation, subjects made their judgments publicly before the rest of the group, but still prior to hearing the other judgments. Deutsch and Gerard reasoned that the subject was more committed to his initial opinion in the magic pad condition that in the no-commitment condition, and most committed of all in the public statement condition. The data came out as expected. Subjects complied the least when they had to give their initial opinion publicly prior to hearing the group's opinion. They complied a moderate amount in the magic pad condition, and most of all in the condition without any prior commitment.

These experiments are oriented towards two quite distinct elements involved in compliance. The Deutsch and Gerard experiment addresses itself to the question of when the subject will comply with the group's judgment. They found that compliance increases with public statement of opinion after the group's judgment, but it decreases with public statement of one's opinion before the group's judgment. On the other hand, the Gerard experiment emphasizes the conflict involved for the subject when faced with a discrepant group judgment and is addressed to the question of what the subject will do after he has resolved this conflict, that is, after he has decided whether to comply or not. His answer is that the subject's behavior is "frozen" by his decision and that whatever factors lead the subject to comply or not, his subsequent behavior will be consistent with that initial decision. In short, Deutsch and Gerard emphasize short-term variables: if the person will decide to comply or not. Gerard emphasizes the long term: what happens after the compliance decision is made.

Obedience: A Special Case of Compliance

Stanley Milgram (1965) has conducted a series of studies on what he refers to as obedience, but what appears to represent a special case of compliance in an Asch-like situation. In the Milgram paradigm there are three people: the experimenter, a confederate, and a naive subject. Under the guise of a bogus experiment, the experimenter requests that the subject shock the confederate. Over a series of trials the voltage of the shock is increased. Milgram's dependent variable is how far the subject is willing to go in shocking the confederate at the insistence of the experimenter. Let us go into a litle more detail of Milgram's procedure.

"The act of administering shock is set in the context of a learning experiment, ostensibly designed to study the effect of punishment on memory. Aside from the experimenter, one naive subject and one accomplice perform in each session. On arrival, each subject is paid $4.50. After a general talk by the experimenter telling how little scientists know about the effect of punishment on memory, subjects are informed that one member of the pair will serve as teacher and one as learner. A rigged drawing is held so that the naive subject is always the 'teacher' and the accomplice the 'learner.' The learner is taken to an adjacent room and strapped into an 'electric chair.' " (Milgram, 1965, p. 245.) Thus, under the guise of a learning experiment, the subject is instructed to shock the victim (i.e., the confederate) whenever the victim makes a mistake. The subject is seated before a bogus shock generator. On this shock generator are thirty switches, and the subject is told that the lowest switch delivers 15 volts and that each sequential switch delivers an additional 15 volts, up to a maximum of 450. Each of the confederate's errors is to be met with an increase of 15 volts in the shock. The confederate responds to the bogus shock with some anguish. Here is the situation as the subject sees it. "Starting with 75 volts, the learner begins to grunt and moan. At 150 volts he demands to be let out of the experiment. At 180 volts he cries out that he can no longer stand the pain. At 300 volts he refuses to provide any more answers ... the experimenter [then] instructs the naive subject to treat the absence of an answer as equivalent to a wrong answer, and to follow the usual shock procedure." (Milgram, 1965, p. 246.) The dependent variable is the number of sequential shocks the subject is willing to deliver. If the subject tries to break off the experiment, as, for example, when the confederate is no longer responding, the experimenter insists that he go on. The final score the subject gets ranges from 0 (when he is not willing to give any shock at all) up to 30 (when he is willing to give all thirty steps of shock).

How far do you think a subject would be willing to go in such an experiment? Or, put another way, what percentage of the subjects do you think would be willing to give the maximum shock asked by the experimenter? In one study (Milgram, 1963), Milgram asked forty psychiatrists the latter question. The psychiatrists predicted that only 0.1% of the subjects would administer the maximum shock to the victim. This is very discrepant with what Milgram actually found. In the study reported (1963), approximately 62% of Milgram's subjects administered the maximum shock. (What was your prediction?)

Milgram has carried out several variations of this basic experimental paradigm, testing such things as the physical proximity of the victim to the subject and the status of the experimenter. All of these studies came out as expected. For example, the closer the victim is to the naive subject, as, for instance, holding on to his arm, the smaller the percentage of subjects willing to deliver the maximum shock. The higher the status of the experimenter, the greater the number of subjects willing to deliver the maximum shock. However, the most interesting part of Milgram's findings unquestionably is the high percentage of people who were willing to deliver the maximum shock—interesting in the sense that it is very surprising. (At least those forty psychiatrists must have been very surprised.) The high level of compliance does not depend on the respectable aura of science at Yale University. Milgram found a similar high level while operating out of a sleezy office in Bridgeport, Connecticut. Milgram's study of obedience has created much discussion in this country, both in and out of the field of psychology. The points of discussion have revolved around the possibilities for generalization from these findings, and some alarm over the ethics of the experimental method.

A number of our students have reported hearing Milgram's findings discussed in synagogues and churches around the country. The specific example of the Nazis involved in eliminating the Jews in Germany during World War II is always brought up in these discussions. Typically observed in court trials of individuals involved in this genocide is what has become almost a cliché—that the person on trial denies any responsibility for his behavior. He insists that he was "only doing his job." The connection with Milgram's paradigm should be obvious. There, too, the individual is harming another person at the insistence of a third, but high-status, person. One might conclude that the subject in the Milgram experiment is essentially absolving himself of any sense of responsibility for having harmed the confederate. He, too, is only doing his job. Some discussants decry any tendency to view the Nazi genocide as a special case of mass insanity, and insist that Milgram's data suggest that such a thing could easily happen again. While the analogy between the two situations is indeed intriguing, at this point we simply do not know the extent to which we can generalize from Milgram's findings. Some people interested in Milgram's findings demand that we do much more research on this issue with the Milgram paradigm. However, another group of people interested in the Milgram findings argue for quite the opposite recommendation. From their point of view, more work should not be done in the Milgram paradigm, and, further, the original experiment should not have been done in the first place.

Milgram's critics are very concerned about the ethics involved in such experimentation. For example, Milgram reports grown men finally breaking into tears when the experimenter continues to insist that they shock the victim. The ethical argument is that such research exceeds tolerable bounds of experimental impact. Milgram's experiments, the argument goes, have too much impact, are too stressful, and, more importantly, may have had a permanent effect on the subjects. In answer, Milgram reports that only 1.3% of his subjects indicated that they were sorry to have participated in the experiment, and 80% indicated that more experiments of that type should be done.

The question of ethics in research is really never very far from the heart and mind of any experimental social psychologist. Indeed, if the person were not interested in people and the human condition, he probably would never have become a social psychologist in the first place. This is undoubtedly one of the reasons why the question of ethics has received so much discussion in the profession. If there is a generalization to be made from all this discussion, i.e., if there is any consensus among social psychologists, then it is probably something like the following. Social psychologists seem to agree that subjects should never leave an experimental setting any worse off (some say, any differently) than they came to it. One of the ways in which researchers effect this is by means of a very elaborate debriefing after the experiment is over. As mentioned in Chapter 1, debriefing often takes as long or longer than the experiment itself. If the subject has undergone some sort of failure experience in the experiment, as with a manipulation of self-esteem or success in problem-solving, then, of course, the debriefing often focuses upon the deception itself and true scores may be revealed to subjects. The need for experimentation (as opposed to correlational study) is often discussed in detail. Subjects' comments and suggestions for improving studies, for lessening the negative effect involved, and so forth, are solicited by the experimenter. Indeed, the final manipulation involved in many experiments has actually been suggested by subjects who took part in pilot work. Nonetheless, the question of ethics in research is not completely soluble. It is a question that needs and deserves continuing attention as long as research is being done. As the reader might suspect, such issues are much discussed among graduate students in psychology, particularly in social psychology.

Milgram's research is also related to questions of methodology in social psychology. We can assume in Milgram's paradigm that practically no one really wants to shock the confederate. Yet 62% of the people are willing to go through the whole sequence of shock. But what would happen if this task were less noxious to the subject? Recall the issue of demand characteristics, previously discussed in Chapter 1. The notion underlying experimental demand is that, if the experimenter makes clear, by subtle means (gestures, facial expressions, or other cues) consciously or unconsciously, what he expects or wants the subject to do in his experiment, the subject is often willing to accommodate him. This point is emphatically made by the Milgram data. If 62% conformed to the expectations of the experimenter in Milgram's study, then we could expect much greater compliance with the experimenter's demands when the task is far less odious. The need for the elimination of demand characteristics in experimental settings is implied quite clearly by the Milgram data.

Gerard's decisional analysis might also be applied to the Milgram data. This analysis perhaps would imply that in Milgram's paradigm, as in Asch's, subjects would either comply with every request to shock or none of the requests. Milgram's data do not fit with such predictions. The data show a simple lessening of effect (fewer people complying) as trials progress. However, Gerard's analysis requires that the decision on the first trial produce dissonance, and perhaps applying a 15-volt shock to another does not do that. If the shock were increased on the first trial or if the subject knew he would be required to go all the way, we would have a better test of the Gerard hypothesis.

RECENT RESEARCH ON COMPLIANCE

The Foot-in-the-Door Technique

The greater the pressure put upon individuals to perform some behavior or to comply with some request, the greater the percentage of individuals who accede. Freedman and Fraser (1966) acknowledged this well-known principle but were more interested in variables which affect compliance under conditions of very little pressure. They carried out two experiments testing the degree of compliance with *minimal pressure*. The principle they were testing is commonly known as the foot-in-the-door, or gradation, technique. The notion is that, if we can get a person to do a little thing that we want him to do, then he will be much more amenable to agreeing to a much larger request later.

In the first experiment the basic paradigm was to induce people to comply first with a small request and then, three days later, make a larger related request. The control subjects simply were asked to comply with the larger request. All contacts were made by telephone with a randomly selected group of subjects from the Palo Alto telephone directory. "At the first contact the experimenter introduced himself by name and said that he was from the California Consumers' Group. In the performance condition he then proceeded: 'We are calling you this morning to ask you a number of questions about what household products you use so that we can have this information for our public service publication, *The Guide.* Would you be willing to give us this information for our survey?' If the subject agreed, she was asked a series of eight innocuous questions dealing with household soaps (e.g., 'What brand of soap do you use in your kitchen sink?') She was then thanked for her co-operation and the contact was terminated." (Freedman and Fraser, 1966, p. 197.) The control group did not have this initial contact.*

In sum, one group of subjects acceded to a small request, answering a series of eight innocuous questions, and the other group was not contacted. Subsequently, both groups were subjected to the identical large request. The experimenter called back, identified himself, and asked if he could come into the subject's home for a (further) survey. He said, "The survey will involve five or six men from our staff coming into your home some morning for about two hours to enumerate and classify all of the household products that you have. They will have to have full freedom in your house to go through the cupboards and storage places. And all this information will be used in the writing of reports for our public service publication, *The Guide.*" If the subject agreed to the request, she was thanked, but told that at that point the experimenter was merely collecting names of people who were willing to take part and that she would be contacted if it were decided to use her in the survey. If she did not agree, she was thanked for her time. This terminated the experiment.

---

*Actually, two other conditions were run: one in which the subject only agreed to have the survey and the experimenter said that he would contact her when she was needed. The second control condition checked on the subject's familiarity with the experimenter and the experimental condition. In this condition, the experimenter introduced himself, described the organization he worked for, and the survey it was conducting, listed the questions he was asking, and then said he was merely calling to acquaint the subject with the existence of his organization. The results of both of these conditions were very similar to those of the control one-contact condition, and we will not discuss them in any detail here.

The results were clear. In the one-contact condition, 22% of the subjects agreed to the large request. In the two-contact condition, 53% of the subjects agreed to the large request, a clear difference between conditions. However, Freedman and Fraser draw attention to two variables which could have influenced these results. One is the fact that the same person made both requests in the two-contact condition. This could have led to some sort of commitment or involvement with the particular person making the request. Having agreed to the small request, the subject might have felt obligated and not want to disappoint the experimenter. This would inflate the degree of compliance in the two-contact condition. A second influence on these data might be the fact that the two requests were extremely similar. Both requests involved or centered around the same survey. These notions led Freedman and Fraser to conduct a second study.

In the second study, the requests were made by two different people. In addition, Freedman and Fraser tested for the effect of the similarity between the issues and the tasks involved in the two requests. There were four experimental conditions, each embracing two requests. For the first request, the subject was asked either to put a small sign in his window extolling traffic safety or keeping California beautiful, or to sign a petition for one of the two issues. Thus, the first request was either a sign or a petition for either safe driving or beauty. Secondly, all subjects were asked to install on their front lawns a very large sign which said, "Drive Carefully." The four experimental conditions are defined in terms of the similarity of the small and large requests along the dimensions of issue and task. The second request was indeed large: "The subject was shown a picture of a very large sign reading 'Drive Carefully' placed in front of an attractive house. The picture was taken so that the sign obscured much of the front of the house and completely concealed the doorway. It was rather poorly lettered." (Freedman and Fraser, p. 200.) The control group was again a one contact group having only the final large request. Freedman and Fraser's data from this second experiment are presented in Table 3-1. As can be seen from the table, approximately 17% of the subjects in the

TABLE 3-1

Percentage of Subjects Complying with a Large Request Following a Small Request (from Freedman and Fraser, 1966)

Issue	Task			
	Similar	N	Different	N
Similar	76.0	25	47.8	23
Different	47.6	21	47.4	19

One-Contact 16.7 (N = 24)

one-contact condition agreed to put up the large sign. In all of the experimental conditions, larger percentages of subjects acquiesced, although three of the four experimental conditions seem to be nearly identical. When the two issues were different (with tasks similar) or the two tasks were different (with issues similar) or both task and issue were different for the two requests, then approximately 47% of the subjects agreed to the request. However, when both issues and both tasks were similar for the two requests, over 75% of the subjects agreed to the request.

Two kinds of explanations are ruled out in these data. For example, the data cannot be explained by a notion that the subject becomes more convinced about the issue as the result of the initial small request. In this experiment the condition with the issues similar but tasks different had no greater percentage of people comply with the second request than with different issues and different tasks. Therefore the similarity of issue by itself had little effect. By the same token, an explanation which centers on the similarity of the tasks (e.g., putting up signs is a good way of expressing one's opinion) also does not explain the data. When the issues were different, for example, there was no difference between task conditions. Freedman and Fraser explain their data with a more general mechanism. They say, "What may occur is a change in the person's feelings about getting involved in action. Once he has agreed to a request, his attitude may change. He may become, in his own eyes, the kind of person who does this sort of thing, who agrees to requests made by strangers, who takes action on things he believes in, who cooperates with good causes." (Freedman and Fraser, 1966, p. 201.) Apparently, the person's attitude about himself has changed. He now thinks of himself as a "doer."

Guilt

A quite different series of studies on the antecedent conditions of compliance are recorded by Freedman, Wallington, and Bless (1967). In a series of three studies they tested the effects of guilt on compliance with a request. In all three studies the subjects were induced to perform some negative behavior: in one study the subject lied about preknowledge of a test that he had worked on; in the other two studies the subject was induced to knock off a table a stack of a thousand thesis notecards. They were then asked if they would like to take part in another study that a different experimenter was running. Freedman, Wallington, and Bless found consistently that guilt over the previous negative behavior induced the subject subsequently to be more likely to comply with the request to take part in another experiment. The authors interpreted this result as an attempt on the part of the subject to expiate the guilt by doing something good. However, they did find that if the subject thought that agreeing to the request would involve interacting with the person whom he sinned against, then he did not comply. In other words, as a result of the guilt over the negative behavior, the subject tried to make it up to the offended other, but not if it meant interacting with him. In these experiements, too, apparently the crucial variable was the subject's attitude about himself. In a sense, the subject apparently viewed himself as basically a good guy who wronged another. Wronging another threatened his favorable self-concept. By now performing a favor, whether for the person he sinned against or not, he became a good guy again. At one level, perhaps, the subject was trying to deny to himself that he was ever a bad guy to begin with. In one study, Freedman, Wallington, and Bless found that the subject was much more likely to agree to a request from an irrelevant other after the guilt manipulation than he was to a request from a person somehow related to the person he had sinned against.

Conformity as an Interpersonal Tactic

Jones (1964) recently published an intriguing book entitled *Ingratiation,* which we recommend (it can be read in its entirety in one evening). He describes a series of studies, carried out in collaboration with his students, in which subjects were told to get others to like them; in short, to ingratiate themselves. We are particularly interested in behavioral or attitudinal compliance here as a device used to ingratiate oneself with others. Jones makes an interesting distinction between ordinary compliance and ingratiating compliance. ". . . The effectiveness of strategic ingratiation depends on clever concealment of the ingratiator's ulterior motive . . . Conformity in the service of ingratiation . . . must appear to be a happy coincidence in order to be successful." (Jones and Gerard, 1967, p. 586.) In line with this, Jones has found that people instructed to ingratiate themselves with another will agree with the other's opinions, but not all of them, lest he be obvious. Subjects of low status will agree on important issues (relevant to status) and disagree on unimportant issues when instructed to ingratiate themselves with a person of higher status. However, when the high status person is ingratiating, he will agree on unimportant issues, but not on important ones (lest he lose his status). Note that if each is trying to ingratiate himself with the other, they should come to overt agreement on all issues.

We know from other research that we like those who share our opinions. The Jones research indicates that everyone accepts this premise and, further, employs the tactic to win favor from others. Part of the tactic, however, is that one does not agree with the other indiscriminately.

Summary

We have been discussing experimental research in some detail. We should also note that the study of compliance has very important practical implications. Often, we simply do not care whether attitude change or private acceptance accompanies this compliance. This is typically the case, for example, when we talk of obeying the law. Society as a whole is not critically concerned whether a given individual believes a particular law is valid or correct. On the other hand, society is very concerned about whether the individual complies with the law. Consider also situations where we would rather have private acceptance accompanying the compliance but are willing to settle for the compliance alone. A mother's view of her daughter's sexual behavior is a case in point. She might feel horrified at the possibility of her daughter being sexually promiscuous. Naturally, she would prefer that her daughter have opinions about this issue similar to her own, but she is willing to settle for simple compliance.

Sometimes we can safely assume that the person already has the attitude in question, but the trick is to get him to behave consistently with the attitude. For example, one of the difficulties in solving the problem of the chronically unemployed is that even when jobs open up specifically for these people one has difficulty enticing them to apply for the jobs. The data indicate that the unemployed want jobs very much. Nonetheless, various factors, like low expectations of being selected for the job, prevent the person from even applying in the first place. Consequently, in this case, the emphasis is on getting him to comply, getting him to behave in a particular way, and little attention is necessary to the private acceptance of such behavior. The same problem holds for some of our more liberal universities which are highly desirous of obtaining a more heterogeneous student body. They find it is often very difficult to get people from particular social or cultural subgroups even to apply for admittance. Again, the focus is on compliance, and private acceptance is of little consequence.

On the other hand, there are a great many practical and theoretical situations where belief, or private acceptance, is of paramount importance. In the next two chapters, we explore this topic of private acceptance more fully.

CHAPTER FOUR

Private Acceptance and Interpersonal Variables

This chapter and the next discuss private acceptance as a dependent variable. The approach is similar to that used in Chapter 3. However, instead of examining whether the group can induce the person to *behave as if* he accepted the group norm or opinion, we will emphasize whether the individual *privately accepts* this group norm. Public behavior is a secondary concern, although the issue will be raised from time to time to compare compliance and private acceptance.

Our discussion of private acceptance has been divided into two parts. This chapter considers the effects of one's relationship to the group. The next chapter stresses the group as a source of information. However, one's relationship to the group and one's use of the group as a source of information cannot always be easily separated, and their division is somewhat arbitrary. Nonetheless, it is still a distinction worth making.

Let us illustrate the difference between the relationship to the group and the group as a source of information with an example. There are two experimental conditions. The subjects in one experimental condition are told that their group of attractive others disagrees with them. The subjects in the second experimental condition are told that a randomly selected batch of peers disagrees with them (or a computer disagrees with them, for that matter). In both cases the subject may change his opinion as a result of our manipulation. In a sense, knowing anyone else's opinion helps to define social reality for us. That they disagree with us may lead us to reassess our own opinion and subsequently to change. This type of influence we might call a cognitive influence. On the other hand, attractive others should have a much greater impact on our subjects' opinions, especially when the relationship to the others is salient. Attractive others would have an effect on private acceptance, beyond that expected on the simple basis of knowing someone else disagreed with you. But the variables may still not be altogether separate. For example, these attractive others might be perceived as more believable sources of information. Perhaps other attractive people whose information cannot be depended on (a young son, for example) would not affect our opinions much. If so, we would want to limit the generalization made above. This theoretical problem will be tackled later, but obviously one can see from our example that the distinction between these two types of influence on private acceptance is not always clear and is upheld mostly for the sake of convenience.

DISTINGUISHING BETWEEN PUBLIC COMPLIANCE AND PRIVATE ACCEPTANCE

Compliance is often mistaken for private acceptance in the research literature, particularly in experiments dealing with the subjects' relationship to the group. Often one cannot tell which dependent variable an investigator is measuring in his experiment. Simply determining whether the measure was a behavioral one or an opinion is not enough to reassure us. In much of the research to be described here, the subject has filled out some attitude scales as the dependent measure. Nevertheless, one's mark on an attitude scale is a form of behavior, and if the individual thinks that the group will see it, he can comply on the attitude scale just as he complies in the Asch situation by saying that line A is longer than line B. The crucial question for distinguishing between compliance and private acceptance in both cases is still whether the subject now *privately* endorses his public attitudinal position or lineal judgment. How does one test for private endorsement? This issue has been considered briefly before. The two experiments to follow illustrate more completely.

Coch and French (1948) provide a neat example of a person publicly conforming but privately rejecting the group norm. They were interested in studying resistance to change in industry, but we will examine the case of an individual person, a clothes presser. This person was placed in a group that had been working together for some time. Apparently the group had developed its own production norms and insisted on conformity to these norms by the group members. At the time the presser joined the group, the rest of the group was producing at the rate of about fifty units an hour. After a couple of weeks, the new girl became accustomed to the work and her production began to rise. She produced more than others in the group. The group moved quickly to enforce its norm and began, in the words of

Coch and French, to "scapegoat" the girl. This scapegoating included several forms of harassment and is not unusual in industrial settings. The authors have seen several instances in unionized shops, in the military service, and in classrooms. At any rate, the enforcement of the group norm was effective. The girl's productivity promptly dropped and subsequently stayed at the same level as the rest of the group. This is the same process that we discussed earlier regarding behavioral deviation from group norms. The girl deviated from the norms; the group communicated to her immediately; she apparently was threatened with psychological rejection from the group, including isolation from the rest of the group; her behavior promptly fell into line with the group norms. At this point, we have no firm evidence whether this was simply public compliance without private acceptance or whether the girl now privately accepted the group norm as the proper level of productivity. Quite accidentally, Coch and French were provided with this evidence. At a later time, the group was broken up and dispersed throughout the factory. When the group was no longer present, i.e., when the girl was no longer under the group's surveillance, her productivity doubled within four days and stabilized at this higher figure.

In this example, there is a clear indication of public compliance without private acceptance. When the group could no longer observe the girl's behavior, the behavior changed dramatically. This is often a good paradigm for studying the difference between public compliance and private acceptance. We simply remove the subject to a position or situation where the group cannot observe her. If her behavior both in and out of the group's presence is quite similar, we can conclude that she has privately accepted the norm. If she behaves differently, we conclude that she is publicly complying with the norm, but has not privately accepted it. Her public behavior would be dependent on the possibility that the group could observe the behavior. Of course, we don't mean that the group must physically observe the behavior, but only that the group be aware of the behavior. This provides a clue about when this paradigm would not be adequate for testing the difference between public compliance and private acceptance.

Whether a person will continue to comply when the group is not present depends partly on whether he feels that the group would be aware of deviant behavior. For example, suppose that the Coch and French clothes presser had become good friends with one of the others in the group. Suppose further that after the group had been dispersed throughout the factory, this person had continued to visit our subject and to chastise her for any deviations from the old group norm. Such behavior from a group representative would likely lead the girl to lower her productivity, perhaps even to match the old group norm. In short, when the subject's behavior could become known to the rest of the group, the Coch and French paradigm does not provide an adequate measure of private acceptance.

An experiment by Gerard (1954) provides us with another way of differentiating between public compliance and private acceptance. Only part of Gerard's experiment is applicable for our purposes here. He varied the attractiveness of discussion groups by telling some subjects that the experimenter was successful in composing a group of people who found one another especially congenial, and telling other subjects that attainment of this criterion was not possible and they would *not* be very congenial. (As we will discuss later, this is a typical and effective way of manipulating attraction to the group.) Each group was made up of people who held similar opinions on the discussion topic. For our present purposes, the major point of this experiment is what happened a week later. In what was described as a second experimental session, each subject was confronted by a confederate who was introduced as a representative of another group. The confederate was trained to argue effectively against various group positions taken on the prior discussion topic, and he argued against the consensus reached in each subject's former group. The dependent variable was the percentage of people who changed their opinions as a result of this attack. Gerard found that the unattracted subjects were much less resistant to attack by the confederate than those more attracted to the group. That is, subjects in the low-attraction condition changed their opinions more in the direction advocated by the confederate than did subjects in the high-attraction condition. Gerard's paradigm provides us with a different way of methodologically differentiating between public compliance and private acceptance. If the person is only publicly complying with the group's norms, then he should drop this cloak when he is under attack out of the group's presence. The relative resistance to persuasive attempts out of the group's presence can serve as an indicator of the degree of prior private acceptance.

Removal of the group and resistance to outside attack are two techniques for assessing the difference between public compliance and private acceptance. They provide us with some assurance of the relative degree to which the subject privately endorses the norm. In many experiments, we do not need to go this far to measure private acceptance effectively. As a minimum, however, we must be certain that the subject is indeed privately responding to the dependent measure. If experimental demands do not indicate to the subject how he *should* respond, and if the subject is confident that the group will *never* see his response, then we have a relatively valid measure of his private acceptance of the group norm. However, in many experiments emphasizing one's relationship to the group, demand characteristics and possible observation by the group cannot be effectively ruled out. In the sections to follow, we will concentrate on studies in which the dependent measure is surely private acceptance. The first independent variable of interest is attraction to the group, sometimes also called the cohesiveness of the group.

ATTRACTION TO THE GROUP

We use the concept "attraction to the group" to imply a property of the individual. One's attraction to the group is simply the degree of positive orientation towards other group members or towards the group as a whole.

Attraction and Cohesiveness

The terms "cohesiveness" and "attraction" are sometimes used interchangeably. However, through the 1940's the term "cohesiveness" was used to describe a group property, rather than an individual's reaction to the group. Presumably several variables independently contributed to the group's cohesiveness, such as: (1) the attractiveness of a group for its members, (2) the coordination of the efforts of the members, (3) the level of motivation of group members to do a task with zeal and efficiency (Golembiewski, 1962). Any one of these variables could affect the cohesiveness of a given group. Today, cohesiveness is commonly defined as "the total field of forces which act on members to remain in the group . . . and may be [operationally] defined as the average for all members of the resultant force toward remaining in the group" (Festinger, Schachter, and Back, 1950). Thus, cohesiveness is still perhaps a group property, although we calculate it by theoretically averaging individuals' "resultant forces." Cohesiveness would include not only the attraction that the group holds for its members but also any other force operating on the individual to stay in the group. As we have discussed before, we find group variables conceptually imprecise and experimentally difficult to work with. Consequently, we will not use the term "cohesiveness," but we will discuss separately each of the variables that presumably contribute to cohesiveness.

Sources of Attraction

Attraction to the group is one of the most frequently manipulated variables in the study of group effects on the individual. Attraction may be varied in several ways. For example, recall the Gerard experiment, in which he varied attraction to the group by telling some groups they would be especially congenial and by telling others that they would not be congenial. This is one way of varying attraction; a little imprecise perhaps, but effective nevertheless. There are a number of other effective ways of manipulating attraction, although they are probably not any more precise. Other methods include telling the subject that the other group members like him, telling the subject that other members have opinions and attitudes similar to his, telling the subject that it is a prestigious group.

Whatever the source of attraction, there seems to be a uniform effect: the more attractive the group is for the individual, the greater the influence that the group is able to exert on him. In short, the greater the attraction, the greater the private acceptance. (There are some exceptions to this, but we will discuss them a little later.) Perhaps most illustrative of the study of attraction on interpersonal influence is an experiment by Kurt Back (1951). Back was interested in how much individuals in dyads could influence one another as a function of their attraction for each other. He varied attraction in three different ways (with high and low attraction conditions within each variation): as one type, he varied the personal attractiveness of the partner (some subjects were told that they would be especially congenial); in another method, he varied the attractiveness of the outcome of the group task (some subjects could win a special prize of $5.00 each); in yet a third manner, he varied the group prestige—the value of belonging to the group (some subjects were told that they had been placed together in a group because they were especially good at the task). In each of the three variations there tended to be greater change produced in the high attraction groups (although the change was not statistically very strong). The ways in which the subjects went about this influence also varied depending on the source of attraction. In the personal attraction variation group members tended to approach their task in a more languid and pleasant fashion. When task attractiveness was varied, the group members tended to try to complete the activity as quickly and efficiently as possible. When group prestige was varied, group members tended to behave quite cautiously and to concentrate on their own actions, apparently to avoid endangering their status.

There are a number of studies on this topic (see Hare, 1962), and almost all of them indicate that greater attraction to the group produces greater private acceptance of the group norms and greater susceptibility to influence by the group. With some exceptions to be noted later, this appears to be as solid an empirical generalization as one can arrive at in social psychology. The question is, however, why should it be true? A number of variables, not mutually exclusive, may contribute to the general effect.

Factors Contributing to the Effect of Attraction on Private Acceptance

Similarity of opinion. When we tell a subject that another person has attitudes or opinions similar to his own, his attraction to the other increases. There is an aspect of psychological implication to this finding. That is, to some extent a person feels that if another person believes the same things he believes, he *ought* to like the other. Heider (1958) has empahsized the phenomenology of the individual subject. He proposes that people in general believe, as a part of our culture, that if they agree with others they should also like them. In Heider's phenomenological terminology, P = the perceiver and O = another person; the statement is phrased as " 'P agrees with O' induces 'P likes O' ." This phenomenological relationship could just as easily work in the other direction. We could say, " '*P* likes *O*' induces '*P* agrees with *O*'." This statement represents a tendency on the part of people to perceive that they should somehow agree with those they like and like those with whom they agree. We suggest that we learn, as a part of our culture, that agreeing with someone and liking someone fit together.

Instrumentality of the opinion response. We assume that the subject has learned in the past that a similarity of opinion may lead to liking. If we are more anxious for attractive others to like us than for unattractive others, then we should change our opinions to agree more with attractive others. Thus, to the notion of psychological implication we add that of instrumentality. This instrumentality is rooted in two assertions: (1) if we believe or act like attractive others, then they will like us more; (2) we have been rewarded in a number of ways in the past for acting as attractive others do. These rewards have been delivered not only by the attractive others, but also by other groups members and outsiders.

Self-definition. Kelman (see Kelman and Eagly, 1965) has suggested that our definition of self is closely connected to the attitudes and opinions we hold and also to our acceptance of influence attempts from others. Thus, in order to view oneself positively (which most people do), one should hold opinions and attitudes similar to those of positive others and dissimilar from negative others. Turning this around, holding opinions similar to positive others and dissimilar from negative others is one way to define the self positively. Changing one's attitudes and opinions so that they are more like positive others and more unlike negative others enhances one's self-view. Kelman calls this tendency a source orientation—to view one's relationship to the other in terms of its relevance to self-definition. He finds that when the source orientation is salient, the subject distorts the position of the other so that the attractive other is seen as holding an attitude more like that of self and the unattractive other is seen as holding an attitude more unlike the self than what really exists. When a group norm is discrepant with the subject's views, we should find two things when questions of self-definition are salient. Under such "norm-sending" conditions, we should find greater change when the group is attractive than when the group is relatively unattractive. However, we should also find great distortion in the system. Under a source orientation, the norm of the attractive group should be perceived as being closer to the attitude of the subject than it actually is, and the norm of the unattractive group should be seen as farther away from the attitude of the subject than it really is. Thus, questions of self-definition have important consequences for private acceptance of group norms.

Attention factors. The empirical effect of an attractive other may also be partly due to attention factors. For several reasons, we may attend more closely to what attractive others tell us—perhaps like a figure and ground effect in perception. We merely have to assume that more attractive others stand out more clearly in our phenomenological field and therefore we pay closer attention to them. Thus, when an attractive other or group disagrees with us, we may be more likely to recognize the disagreement (and, hence, change our opinion) than when a less attractive other disagrees with us.

Credibility. If an individual has learned to pay attention to some attractive others in the past, then this may lead to a heightened credibility and trustworthiness of more attractive others as communicators in general. When an attractive other disagrees with us, we are not only more likely to recognize the disagreement, but we would also probably assume that what he says is the truth (or represents social reality, or is more trustworthy) than when the less attractive other says the same thing. The attitude change literature (see Zimbardo and Ebbesen) shows that heightened credibility or trustworthiness of the communicator has a powerful effect on opinion change. In a limited sense, the group can also be viewed as a communicator, with an opinion (e.g., a norm) and a desire to convince others (recall how the group communicated to the deviate in Schachter's experiment, for example). Credibility or trustworthiness may be one of the several factors contributing to the empirical effect of attraction on private acceptance.

Theoretical Issues Related to Attraction

The theories of Kelman and Festinger. Attraction has been a central variable in many theoretical descriptions of private acceptance. However, two important theories, those of Kelman (1958) and Festinger (1953), have somewhat different things to say about the effects of attraction on private acceptance. Festinger distinguishes two main variables in the study of interpersonal influence. They are the same two dependent variables that we have discussed here—compliance and private acceptance. Festinger says a large number of variables (e.g., coercion) produces compliance, but only one variable leads to private acceptance, and that is attraction to the other. According to Festinger, only when one is attracted to the influencing other does one internalize the influence attempt, or norm in question. Indeed, as indicated above, a number of experiments show private acceptance under conditions of high attraction to the other.

Kelman, on the other hand, has an additional refinement of this theoretical model, and one that has not received adequate test as yet. Kelman distinguishes among three forms of interpersonal influence: compliance, identification, and internalization. Kelman uses the term "compliance" in the same way that we and Festinger have done. However, he makes a distinction between types of private acceptance. The term "identification" refers to those conditions under which the person's acceptance of the influence attempt is dependent on his relationship to the other. Kelman makes the same prediction that we have here: highly attractive others produce greater private acceptance—or identification, in

Kelman's terms. But Kelman goes on to say that such private acceptance is not nearly so "permanent" as we have implied. He suggests that the change produced by the attractive other is dependent upon the relationship to the other. If the relationship changes, so should the attitude, with the subject presumably returning to the opinions and attitudes he formerly held. For Kelman, only internalization produces "true" acceptance. However, for internalization to occur, the *content* of the influence attempt—whether it be a particular norm, behavior, or opinion—must fit with the subject's previously formed value system (although one might wonder how one gets the value system in the first place).

The point of interest here is the discrepancy between the theoretical treatment of private acceptance by Kelman and Festinger. Festinger says simply that the variable mediating private acceptance is the attractiveness of the influencing other, and adds that most other variables produce compliance without private acceptance. Kelman agrees with the statement about compliance but maintains that the attractiveness of the influencing other does not mediate true private acceptance. In Kelman's model, private acceptance produced by an attractive other depends on the continuation of the relationship with the other. If this relationship should change, the attitudes and behaviors acquired through the relationship should be abandoned. Before drawing any firm conclusions, let us look at a related theory, that of French and Raven.

French and Raven's theory of social power. The term "social power" has often been used in the psychological literature, but it is difficult to distinguish from that of conformity. One may define social power as "the degree to which a person or group may influence the opinions or behavior of another person in a particular situation." As stated, the principal difference between social power and conformity is that the term "power" emphasizes the *influencer* and the term "conformity" refers to the behavior of the *influencee.* In both cases, however, the dependent variable is the same: the change in the behavior of the recipient of the influence attempt. Consequently, these data about social power are central to the present discussion.

French and Raven (1959) are the major theoreticians about social power. They distinguish among five bases of social power. Each basis or source of power is specific to a particular relationship between two people (let's call the two people X and Y). The five bases of power are quite similar to variables we have already discussed.

The first source or type of power French and Raven call *reward power.* The degree of reward power that X is able to exert over Y depends on X's ability to mediate rewards for Y. As such, reward power may be related to attraction (but also to pressure for compliance). The second type of power, called *coercive power,* is dependent on X's ability to mediate punishments for Y. This is related to what we previously discussed as the degree of external pressure for compliance. A third type, *legitimate power*, depends on Y's perception that X has a right to prescribe his behavior. The fourth type, *referent power*, is based on Y's identification with X and is also closely related to attraction. The last type of power that French and Raven distinguish is called *expert power,* and depends on Y's perception that X has some special knowledge or expertise.

French and Raven discuss when the various types of power will produce compliance and when they will produce private acceptance. As with Kelman and Festinger, French and Raven also suggest that both reward power and coercive power lead to compliance without private acceptance. They do not go into detail about the effects of legitimate, referent, and expert power. However, they do say that effects of these sources of power do not depend on X being able to observe Y. Apparently, French and Raven believe that expert, referent, and legitimate power each affects private acceptance.

A theoretical integration. Kelman emphasizes his process of internalization as the only variable affecting "true" private acceptance. For private acceptance to occur, according to Kelman, the information and norms being transmitted must fit with the subject's previously formed value system. Festinger, on the other hand, is convinced that the crucial variable underlying private acceptance is attraction to the other. He feels that when one is highly attracted to another, one accepts the norms and values transmitted by the other, but that *other* variables produce only compliance without private acceptance. French and Raven seem to feel that legitimate power, referent power, and expert power produce private acceptance, but coercive power and reward power do not. This sounds like quite a discrepancy among the three positions. What would it take to integrate these three theoretical approaches?

Two assumptions are necessary to integrate the three approaches. First, if legitimate power, referent power, and expert power increased Y's attraction to X (and reward power and coercive power did not), then French and Raven's theoretical treatment of power would fit quite neatly with Festinger's discussion of compliance and private acceptance. Second, if we also assume that to some extent (or under some conditions) the effect of attraction to the other depends on a continued relationship with him, then Kelman's theoretical scheme might fit neatly with the other two.

Both assumptions have to be valid or at least one of the theories is wrong. The first assumption seems reasonable enough, but what about the second? When is a continued relationship necessary to maintain private acceptance and when is it not? We simply don't know, but let us offer one possible hypothesis.

As we shall discuss later, under the concept of functional autonomy of motives, behavior performed over a period of time tends to acquire motivating characteristics of its own. Thus, people who join a group for one particular reason often subsequently find (perhaps through a process of distortion) other attractive aspects of group membership. Consequently, long after the original motive for joining the group is inactive, membership is still continued and found attractive. This process of seeking other justifications for group membership takes time.

A similar process might affect the relationship between attraction to the other and private acceptance. Suppose we have changed our opinions or behavior as a result of our relationship with the attractive other at some time in the past. Suppose further that this relationship with the attractive other has changed, i.e., the other is no longer so attractive. The question may be asked, what are the conditions under which this opinion and behavior change will be stable and not dependent upon the continuation of the relationship? If the present analysis is correct, it would be related to the amount of time that has elapsed since the opinion or behavior change. If some time has elapsed, then we may have acquired other justifications for holding the opinions or performing the behavior. Under that condition, even though the relationship with the other may have changed, our opinions and behavior may continue. However, if little or no time has elapsed since this change occurred, the *change* in the relationship to the formerly attractive other may be especially salient. Consequently, a change in the relationship with the other might also lead us to abandon our new opinions and behavior. Of course, we are not suggesting that time itself is the crucial variable. The psychological variable involved is the number and importance of other justifications one has acquired for one's opinions and behavior—which would ordinarily (but not always) be related to time. This justification hypothesis has not been tested, however.

Status

The term "status" may be defined as "the worth of a person as estimated by a group or class of persons. The estimate of worth is determined by the extent to which his attributes or characteristics are perceived to contribute to the shared values and needs of the group or class of persons." (Secord and Backman, 1961, p. 294-95.) To discuss status reasonably we clearly have to delineate the group presumably conferring the status. This group may be extremely small, such as a gang, or as large as a society. Obviously, the attributes contributing to status within a given group must not be too common. Most people distinguish three bases or types of factors which contribute to status. First, status is conferred upon those who provide rewards for the rest of the group and whose contribution is crucial to the group goal. A member of a gang who is bright enough to plan robberies effectively is given especially high status. His planning ability is crucial—the other gang members would not receive any reward from the group effort without it.

A second basis for status is the costs incurred by the individual in the realization of the group goal. To continue the gang example, the individual who holds out against intense police questioning should be held in high esteem and given special privileges within the group. A third basis for the attribution of status to another is the investments of the other. Investments (see Homans, 1950) refer to any attribute or possession of the individual which is positively viewed by the rest of the group. Investments could include such things as age, height (especially among school boys), tenure at a given job, experience at the work in question, and so forth. Each of these three factors—reward value for the group, costs incurred, and investment—contributes to the status conferred upon an individual by a particular group. In the following two sections we will look at the effects of status and private acceptance from two perspectives. First, we will inspect the effect of variations in the status of the other on our private acceptance. Second, we will look at the effects of the status of self in the private acceptance of influence attempts from the other.

Status of the other. Research abounds on the effects of the other's status on private acceptance. However, there are two sources of contamination in this research. In the first place, this is one of the areas in which there has been a good deal of confusion between private acceptance and compliance. In the second place, status is typically not manipulated. Instead, status is often allowed to vary freely and is therefore confounded with other variables of theoretical interest. In spite of all this theoretical and methodological ambiguity, the data are still quite uniform: the higher the status of the other, the greater the private acceptance (and compliance) on the part of the recipient of the communication or norm. Let us look at other variables confounded with status.

Ordinarily, we would expect that the greater the status of the other, the greater his attractiveness. Of course, enhanced attractiveness should also increase private acceptance. In addition, the greater the status of the other, the greater his credibility or trustworthiness. Increased credibility, too, would lead to private acceptance. On these grounds, we would expect that high status of the other should consistently produce private acceptance. However, it is not clear whether the other's status has an independent effect, or whether it is mediated through some related process, such as attractiveness or increased credibility of the high-status other.

The individual also tends to distort the situation when confronted with a high-status other. Pepitone (1950) investigated such distortion effects directly. In his study, male high school students were interviewed by three adults. Subjects expected that on the basis of this interview they might be able to receive a ticket to a basketball game. Pepitone varied the roles that the panel of interviewers enacted. On one dimension, he varied the friendliness that a particular interviewer evidenced toward the subject. On another dimension, he varied the apparent power of the interviewer to determine whether the ticket was given or not. The results were as predicted. The subject distorted the situation so that it appeared to be more in his favor than actually was the case. That is, the friendly interviewer was viewed as having greater power than he actually had. Conversely, the unfriendly interviewer was viewed as having less power than he actually had. The other dimension worked in a similar manner. The high-power person was viewed as friendlier than he actually was, and the low-power person was viewed as less friendly than he actually was. The future appears to be rosy.

Thibaut and Riecken (1955) also report an effect of status on interpersonal distortion—this time, the distortion of the perceived causality of the other's behavior. In their experiment, the subject attempted to influence two confederates whose status was varied. One confederate, dressed very neatly, was introduced as a Ph.D. and a new instructor at the college. The other confederate, dressed very casually, was introduced as a freshman. Assigned the role of communicator, the subject tried to convince the others to donate blood for a Red Cross drive. After some hesitancy, both confederates complied and agreed to contribute. One dependent variable was the perceived causal locus for the compliance: whether the behavior was self-caused or induced by the subject. The results are very interesting. The high-status other was viewed as self-directed. After compliance, the subject liked the high-status other more and saw his acquiescence as internally caused rather than caused by the subject. On the other hand, the compliance of the low-status other was perceived as being directly affected by the subject's communication, as externally caused, and the subjects liked him less.

As a last form of distortion with reference to status, we might expect that when a high-status person communicates to us vis-a-vis our discrepant behavior, we distort his position on the issue. That is, a subject should perceive less disagreement between his position and that of the high-status other than between his position and that of a low-status other, much as Kelman and Eagly found with attractive others.

Empirically, then, the effects of the status of the other are quite consistent. A high-status other produces greater private acceptance and greater compliance than a low-status other. In addition, we distort his position and behavior so as to fit our preconceptions of one deserving of such status. The data and issues relating to one's own status are a little more complicated.

Status of self. The data with regard to status of self seem to be contingent upon both the situation and the role that a person must play in the group. Depending on these variables, sometimes the high-status individual changes more, sometimes less. The same is true of compliance. Sometimes the high-status person complies with the group norms more, sometimes less. There is such confusion between compliance and private acceptance that perhaps both variables warrant detailed discussion.

First of all, what about compliance? Several points should be made. It seems clear that the high-status person cannot deviate *too* much from the group norms in his overt behavior, or he would be demoted or rejected. However, the high-status person is seen as more responsible for the correctness of the group's behavior. As a result, if the group is headed in the wrong direction, the high-status person should deviate from the group's norms in order to entice the group to change (partly to preserve his status?). If a group is failing at a task, the status hierarchy tends to be changed (Hamblin, 1958). It is as if the group were searching for a new leader to cope with a difficult and frustrating situation. On the other hand, Hollander (1958) suggests that a high-status person builds up "idiosyncrasy credit"; i.e., he is *allowed* to deviate more than other group members as a result of previous compliance. Idiosyncrasy credit is like a psychological bank account—deviation reduces one's credit, and too much deviation exhausts the balance. A negative balance leads to rejection or demotion.

In a given compliance situation, the behavior of the high-status person apparently depends entirely on his perception of what is going on in the group at the time. For example, he will comply more than other group members to a discrepant group norm if he perceives that compliance is good for the group, and less than others if he perceives it as bad for the group. Medow and Zander (1965) found the high-status person to be more involved with the group's goals, to be more concerned that the group be correct, and to perceive that he has greater influence over the group than other group members do. If the high status person thinks the group is incorrect, he should be more motivated than the other group members to take action to change the group's norms and behavior. But in order to influence the group, he must deviate. This suggests a complex relationship between status and compliance. When there is no clear evidence that the group is wrong in its norm or judgment, then we should get a monotonically positive relationship between status and compliance: the greater the status of the subject, the greater his compliance to the group norm. However, when it becomes increasingly obvious that the group is incorrect, the behavior of the high-status person is affected more than any other (since he has a greater stake in the group and can influence it more). When the group is wrong, then the high-status person should deviate, whereas the behavior of members of lower status should be less affected.

Each of these relationships has been reported in the literature under conditions that we interpret as being correct or incorrect group norms. However, there has been no direct test of this hypothesis.

The effects of one's own status on private acceptance are also not well researched. It follows from our previous discussion, however, that a high-status person would ordinarily not be too concerned if he disagreed with a low-status person. If high-status people do not attend to disagreement much, then they should seldom be compelled to reassess their attitudinal position. If we wish to speculate about the conditions underlying attitude change for high-status people, then we should probably search for factors which would lead the high-status person to focus on the disagreement and perhaps reassess his attitudinal position, thereby leading to possible change and private acceptance. Although the high-status person is not often directly influenced by others, he could be influenced under one or more of the following conditions. (1) The high-status person should be influenced when all of the group disagree with him. (2) He should be influenced also when the disagreement between himself and others is crucial in attaining the group goal. (3) The high-status person should be influenced when there has been recent disagreement within the group on other issues, rendering the individual's status somewhat unstable. (4) The high-status person should be influenced when the group is threatening to dissolve. Although the list is not exhaustive, each of these factors should produce a feeling of instability about one's status. As a result, the disagreement with others ought to become more important and force one to inspect and perhaps reassess his attitudinal position. The same factors might also lead to greater compliance.

The positive effects of status instability on the acceptance of influence are sometimes limited because of communication difficulties among group members. Kelley (1951) and Cohen (1958) investigated patterns of communication within groups when status was experimentally varied. In general, they found that high-status people communicated less to the low-status people than vice-versa. Moreover, Cohen (1958) found that people of unstable high status communicated even less to low-status people than did the high-status people whose position was stable. The person of high but unstable status appears to be attempting to re-establish his position in the group (at least from his own perspective) by setting himself apart from the rest of the group. By decreasing his communication to the rest of the group, the high-status person presents himself as one "different" from the others in the group. This hypothesis is quite discrepant with the ones discussed in the previous paragraph. However, we suggest a possible, but yet untested, resolution. Perhaps when a person's status is only mildly threatened, he is alerted to disagreements with others, attends more closely to the disagreements, and possibly subsequently reassesses his position. In this view, a very mild threat to status merely increases one's attention to the others in his field. However, when the threat to one' status is more severe, the attentional factor is swamped by an extreme concern for one's position. To re-establish himself in his own eyes as somewhat different from the others, he behaves in a way that cuts him off from the others. If so, the behavior of a person whose high status is severely threatened is self-defeating. Cutting oneself off from others, responding less to their communications, and differentiating oneself more from them should lead to even greater instability, if not the downfall of the high-status person. Sound like anyone you know?

OTHER VARIABLES

Motivation for Group Goals

Motivation for group goals inevitably contributes to the continuation of the group and presumably mediates the private acceptance of group norms. Of course, often a group has more than one goal, or perhaps a primary goal and several secondary goals. In addition, the group members may not agree on which goal is the primary one. For example, what is the group goal of a bowling team? To identify it, we would first have to determine the motivations of the individual members of the group. On one team, all the members may view bowling as a competitive sport, and their primary motivation within the group may be to win. For another bowling team, the members' motivation may simply be a night out on the town, and winning may be secondary. Probably winning and social interaction are goals of both teams in the example. But we can illustrate the difference in the effect of the primary goals on the group by the following. Suppose that one of the members on each team appears intentionally not to be doing very well. The team motivated by winning would be more annoyed by this behavior—openly derogating or rejecting the intentional goof-off—than would the "night out" team. Even if the bowler is really having an off night and is not intentionally trying to do badly, the "winning" team is still more likely to infer that he is not trying hard enough. They would infer that it is intentional interference with the group goal, even when it is not. The situation would be reversed if someone were bowling adequately but were socially surly. In that case, he is more likely to be communicated to about this behavior, told he is not trying hard enough, or rejected by the "night out" team than by the "winning" team.

Group goal is too simple a notion as we have presented it. Not everyone in a group defines the group goal in the same way. It varies from person to person. In our example of the team motivated by competition, not everyone in that group would be equally motivated to win. A person's perception of the group goals depends on his individual goals for group membership—the reasons why he originally joined the group and the reasons why he is staying in it. Consequently, the reactions to the surly bowler in the example above would vary from person to person, depending on how the individual perceived the group goal and whether or not he personally endorsed it. In short, it is tempting to be superficial about the topic of group goals, but when analyzing a group, one must be very careful to know exactly what its goals are. The analysis of group goals often depends less on the formal organization and characteristics of the group than it does on how the individual members of the group perceive these goals.

Functional autonomy of motives. A person may join a group because the group is instrumental in achieving some particular goal for him. Over a period of time, however, he may find other attractive and rewarding aspects of the group membership. Through interaction, the group membership has become an end in itself—the motive for membership has become functionally autonomous—and continued membership no longer depends on the original motive (Gordon Allport, 1937). Whether or not the motives underlying the group membership become functionally autonomous depends partly on whether the person can keep his individual goal specifically in mind while a member. Tsouderos (1955) has suggested that the less specialized the role in a (voluntary) organization, the more likely the individual is to view membership as a positive goal in itself. In his study, Tsouderos found that people who had highly specialized roles regarded their group membership as a means to an end. Without a specific and clear-cut goal to keep in mind while interacting with the group, the individual is thrown back on the group membership and other members to seek out rewards for his behavior. For example, "in a laboratory experiment using discussion groups, Wolff (1953) observed that members in a group where the chairman approved of their remarks based their liking for the group on the evident worth of their contributions, while members of groups where the chairman devalued their comments liked the group because of the persons in the group and the interesting topics discussed." (Quoted from Cartwright and Zander, 1960, p. 77; see also the discussion in Chapter 5 on dissonance theory.)

An individual's present motives for group membership are not necessarily the same as those which originally led him to join the group. Motives for membership may change drastically over time. However, since the individual's motives tend to become functionally autonomous, so may the group's reason for being. The group's mainspring for existence—the group's goals—may also become functionally autonomous over time. To change the goals of a group, we should first specify what the existing goals are. In doing so, one must not assume that the original goals are still the prime motivations for individual members or the group as a whole.

Group goals and attraction. Kurt Lewin once said that the attractiveness (or valence, as he put it) of membership in a group may be quantified as equal to the attractiveness of the group's goal multiplied by the probability that the group will reach the goal. This means that when either the attractiveness of the goal or the probability of reaching the goal is low, then the resulting attractiveness of the group will also be low. For the attractiveness of the group to be high, both the attractiveness of the goal and the probability of reaching the goal must be high. A study by Deutsch (1959) revealed that the members became more attracted to a group if they were told that the group had a higher probability of achieving its goal. However, to apply Lewin's equation, we must be able to identify the group goal and, as we have indicated, this is not a simple task sometimes. We will return to the question of motivation for group goals and its effect on influence in our discussions below.

The Interdependence of Group Members.

Interdependency of group members leads to greater compliance. The more interdependent the group members in achieving some goal, the more compliance the group can produce to norms, particularly those norms instrumental to achieving the goal. This is partly explicit social exchange—a group member thinks that he is trading-off his behavioral compliance for the greater good, the group goal.

Interpendence of group members also leads to increased attraction for one another (Grinker and Spiegel, 1945). Since it is attractive, an interdependent group should also produce private acceptance, in addition to the compliance noted above. So, we conclude that interdependence of group members leads to greater influence of the group on the individual, both publicly and privately. But why? What causes or mediates the effect? Compliance might be explained by the concept of social exchange, but what about private acceptance? If increased attractiveness is mediating private acceptance, then we would expect interdependent groups also to be able to influence members on issues unrelated to specific group norms. However, if attraction is the *crucial* variable, then interdependence of group members *per se* should have little effect on private acceptance. This means that if we could vary the interdependence of group members while keeping their attraction for one another constant, we should find that highly interdependent groups could not influence their members' private attitudes any more than less interdependent groups. To our knowledge, such issues have never received adequate test.

The concept of "common fate" is closely related to that of interdependence. Common fate usually describes a "we're in this together" attitude, or a positive feeling towards another as a function of having shared some difficult situation. Common fate may include such things as having gone on a peace march together or having been in the same platoon in combat. As a theoretical construct, common fate has received little empirical work, but its effects are probably similar to those of interdependence, in the sense that they may also depend on the intervening variable of attraction.

"Interdependence" and "common fate" are terms typically used to refer to groups. Both terms imply a symmetrical relationship—group members are *equally* interdependent; individuals *share* a common fate. Interdependence and common fate can be subsumed under the more general term "dependency." Dependency can refer both to groups and to individuals, and it allows for asymmetrical relationships. That is, person A can be more dependent on person B than vice versa. The greater dependency of A on B, the greater the ability of B to influence A (but not vice versa). If we are dependent on another, we not only lean on him as a source of information about social reality, but in exchange we are also willing to comply with his wishes.

It is interesting to ask when and how a person will reject the dependent role. Witness the position of a teenager who is still dependent in many respects on his parents but whose primary peer group decries dependency as a negative attribute. In overtly attempting to weaken the dependent relationship, the teenager may adopt behavior clearly divergent from the expectations of his parents and may also try to develop attitudes and opinions which are different from those of his parents. The behavior of the teenager suggests several interesting areas of research. We might look into the variables contributing to the acceptance of a dependent role, the conditions under which the person will attempt to break off the dependent relationship, and the strategies he employs to dissolve the relationship. We note that the teenager's often bizarre behavior has a dual function, although he may not realize it. It not only helps to define his self-image as an independent person, but it also provides cues to the other—in this case the parents—that the dependent relationship is no longer desired. Indeed, the cues provided to the other that the relationship is no longer desired may be the most important part of this behavior.

Positive Appraisal outside of the Group

When outsiders value a group positively at least three things happen for the individual. First, other members of the group appear more positive to him. This is partly a simple communication effect, in that he is accepting the opinion of others about the group. Second, we can assume that positive appraisal is rewarding and that the person seeks to have that reward applied to him. He should therefore want to join the group and continue his membership. Third, the individual is likely to relate this positive appraisal to aspects of his own self-definition, as we discussed before. When a person is accepted by an exclusive organization such as a country club or any other private club, there appears to be a relief that is uncorrelated with the attractiveness of the members of the club. It is more clearly associated with the problem of self-definition. As an outsider, he himself endowed the group with positive value and, upon acceptance, appears to be telling himself, "I am indeed that sort of person."

Consequently, we would expect the others' appraisal of our group to have a strong effect on the ease with which the group can influence us, both publicly and privately. The variables of the attractiveness of the group, reward for self, and positive self-identification all work together and in the same direction. Highly esteemed clubs, organizations, universities, and even neighborhoods have powerful effects on those who belong and those who aspire to do so.

Commitment to Future Interaction.

Consider the typical group experiment in the laboratory. A person is interacting with one or more people whom perhaps he has never seen before. He isn't quite certain how the others are reacting to the events affecting them all. However, the experiment will be over in an hour and he senses that he will never see them again. How does this fact, that he is not committed to any future interaction with the others in the group, affect his behavior in this group setting and his reactions to the others?

This is an important consideration because so many of our experimental data on groups (and conformity) are based on just such fleeting interactions. A number of investigators, particularly sociologists, have argued that one cannot generalize from short-term groups to groups of long standing in the real world. They cite numerous differences between long-term and short-term groups and their consequences for variables such as conformity.

Of course, short- and long-term groups differ in many ways that are relevant to conformity. People in long-term groups know each other better, have interacted longer, probably like each other better, have better developed norms and sanctions, and so forth. Each of these variables is related to the study of conformity and each is a natural and probable consequence of people interacting over time.

Suppose we found that we could not generalize from short-term groups to long-term ones—for example, that a variable producing one effect in short-term groups leads to an entirely different effect in long-term groups. How could we explain this? Well, there are so many differences between short-term and long-term groups that we could probably offer a number of plausible explanations. In studying such a complex situation, we would prefer to gain more experimental control; to avoid having so many things varying at once. How could we do this? One method is simply to vary the *anticipation* of future interaction rather than the amount or kind of interaction itself. That is, we look at differences between people who anticipate future interaction with one another and those who do not. This way, we can neatly control for such obviously important variables as the amount of interaction the members have with one another, how friendly they have been, how well they know each other, and so forth. The only difference between the two is that one group would anticipate, or be committed to, future interaction. Loosely speaking, a group anticipating future interaction may well *define* itself as a long-term group and the group not anticipating future interaction may define itself as a short-term group. Varying commitment to future interaction has two important advantages: (1) we can manipulate it in the laboratory; (2) as a result, we can test the generalizability of the laboratory findings based on fleeting interactions. As we shall see below, commitment to future interaction does indeed have important consequences for conformity, with regard both to compliance and to private acceptance.

A study by Kiesler and Corbin (1965) illustrates the effect of commitment to future interaction on private acceptance. They were specifically concerned with the interactive effects of commitment and attraction to the group. Recall that typically the more attracted an individual is to a group, the more influenced he is by it when he and the group disagree. Kiesler and Corbin argue that this is not always true; there is not always greater private acceptance with increasing attraction. According to them, the positive relationship occurs only when the person does not anticipate any future interaction with the group. Why? Let us take the case of the low-attraction subject as an example. He is interacting with people whom he does not like (and who, typically, do not like him), and with whom he disagrees. A very awkward situation, but how can he resolve it? Kiesler and Corbin maintain that he resolves the situation by divorcing himself from the group. The subject devalues the group and psychologically withdraws from it. That is, he no longer considers himself a member of the group. Consequently, the group has little impact on this subject.

Now, let us take up the case of those subjects who, by manipulation, like the other group members. These subjects disagree with people whom they find highly attractive, and it would not be easy to devalue the attractive others. They reassess their opinions and are likely to change their opinions to bring them more into line with those of attractive others. In sum, the greater the attraction, the greater the impact of the group on the individual. This would be a positive relationship, and it is what usually occurs for subjects who are not committed to future interaction.

What happens when the person expects to interact with the group over a longer period of time, say several sessions? Kiesler and Corbin suggest that this is a very different situation, particularly when the subject does not find the rest of the group attractive. When the unattracted person is not committed to future interaction, he presumably withdraws and bides his time until the experimental hour has elapsed. However, when he must continue the interaction over several sessions, it would be difficult for him to devalue the others and withdraw. When committed to future interaction, our subject is still disagreeing with unattractive others, true—but they are people he must continue to face in the future. To reject or devalue the group under these circumstances would merely increase his discomfort. He would have to continue to interact with an even less valued group. Kiesler and Corbin felt that the effect of commitment to future interaction would be limited to relatively unattracted subjects. Presumably, subjects more attracted to other group members effectively deal with the conflict and the anticipation of future interaction would not be critical. If the effect were limited largely to unattractive subjects, then the overall relationship between attraction and private acceptance would be a U- or a V-shaped one. Decreasing attraction would produce less private acceptance down to a certain point. Beyond that point, decreasing attraction further would actually increase private acceptance.

In their experiment, Kiesler and Corbin varied both the anticipation of future interaction and attraction to the group. All subjects were told that they would have to participate in four experimental sessions. Commitment to future interaction was varied by telling subjects in half the groups that they had a very small chance of changing to a different group if they were dissatisfied (1 in 20, or 5% chance), while the other half of the subjects were told that they had a very good chance of changing groups if they were dissatisfied (19 in 20, or 95% chance). Thus, subjects in the former condition were more committed to continue the interaction with the same group than subjects in the latter condition.

Attraction to the group was varied by manipulating the individual's acceptance by the group. This was done by what we refer to as "the wastepaper basket technique." At an early point in the experiment, the six subjects in each group completed graphic rating scales indicating how much they liked each of the others and how much they thought each of the others would contribute to a good group decision. (Each person thought he was taking part in a study of group decision-making.) The experimenter leafed through these ratings and then threw them in the wastepaper basket, casually remarking that no one had been rejected. At a later point in the experiment, when the experimenter was supposedly compiling a group consensus, he mentioned that subjects might be interested in looking at others' ratings of them.

Fictitious ratings had been made up in advance and were also in the wastepaper basket. The experimenter retrieved the fictitious ratings and passed them out, while mentioning what the average rating seemed to be. One third of the subjects received ratings considerably below average, one third of the subjects approximately average, and one third much above average. This technique has been shown to be a reliable method for systematically varying attraction to the group. Of course, it depends on the principle that we like others who like us and dislike others who dislike us.

Discrepancy in opinion between the subject and the group was held constant from subject to subject. This was done in the following manner. At the beginning of the experiment, the subjects had ranked ten abstract paintings according to their aesthetic appeal. These rankings were allegedly to form the basis for a subsequent group decision. Later, the experimenter gave each subject the "group consensus." To ensure a constant discrepancy, the rankings were systematically manipulated. Regardless of how the subject had ranked the paintings, his sixth choice was made the group's first choice, and his ranks 1-5 were made 2-6 (ranks 7-10 remained unchanged). This is illustrated in Table 4-1. Thus, no matter how an individual arrayed the paintings, the discrepancy between his opinion and that of the group was constant from subject to subject. The dependent variable was the degree to which he re-evaluated his sixth-ranked painting (F) more positively on a second private ranking.

The methodology of second rankings in experiments on private acceptance should be reviewed briefly. Two considerations are especially important. First, the subject must be assured that the group will not see his second ranking or the dependent measure might be one of compliance rather than private acceptance. Second, the subject must not be aware that the investigator is interested in opinion change. That is, he must avoid any

Table 4-1

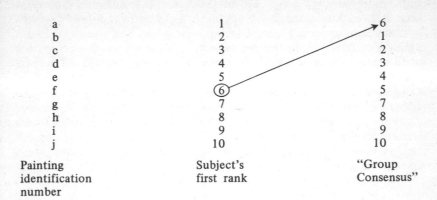

Painting identification number	Subject's first rank	"Group Consensus"
a	1	6
b	2	1
c	3	2
d	4	3
e	5	4
f	⑥	5
g	7	7
h	8	8
i	9	9
j	10	10

implication that he expects or would like to see the subject change his opinion in any particular way (recall our discussion of demand characteristics). Kiesler and Corbin stressed repeatedly to the subjects that the second ranking was a private one and that no one in the group would see it. In fact, the experimenter showed an envelope in which he was going to put the rankings and immediately send them to his superiors. Not only would the other group members not see the individual subject's second rankings, the experimenter would not either. In addition, subjects were identified by number rather than by name, assuring anonymity. To provide an excuse for a second ranking, each subject was given a "guide to modern painting" written specifically for the experiment. To avoid any systematic effects of the guide on opinion change, however, the guide was "fact-free," filled with jargon, and of no help in ranking the paintings. It did, however, allow the experimenter to say, "Now that you have new information and time to consider the paintings further, we would like you to rank them again, just for the Institute." The use of such a device or excuse is common in experiments involving a pretest and a posttest.

To summarize the Kiesler and Corbin experiment, half the subjects expected to continue the interaction over several sessions, half did not. Independently of this manipulation, one third of the subjects were highly attracted to the group, one third about average, and one third considerably below average. The dependent variable was the change in opinion after disagreement with the group. (The subjects, of course, were elaborately debriefed.)

The data are represented in Fig. 4-1 and are arrayed as Kiesler and Corbin had predicted. When the subjects were not committed to future interaction, the less attracted they were to the group, and the less the group was able to influence them, as others had found. As expected, the effect of commitment to future interaction was largely limited to those subjects who found the group unattractive—it had little effect on subjects who found the group either very attractive or just average. (The differences between committed and uncommitted subjects for these two conditions does not approach significance.) Figure 4-1 shows, however, that the group had a considerable effect on unattracted subjects only when they were committed to future interaction with the other group members. For subjects committed to future interaction, the relationship between attraction and influence was U- or V-shaped, as predicted. Kiesler, Zanna, and De Salvo (1966) continued this line of research and found that the opinion change obtained (under conditions of little attraction and commitment to future interaction) was even resistant to subsequent attack. Such resistance to attack assures us that subjects in the experiment were not just complying, but were privately accepting the group's opinion.

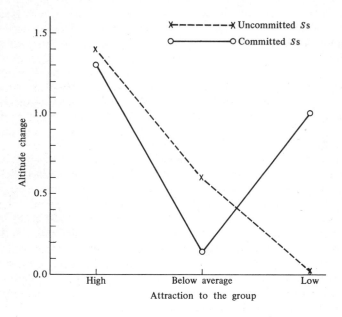

Fig. 4-1.   The relationship of attraction to the group and commitment to continue in the group in conformity to group norms. (From Kiesler and Corbin, 1965.)

Commitment to future interaction had a dramatic effect upon private acceptance and its relationship to attractiveness of the group. The simple positive relationship between attraction and influence obtained in laboratory studies may be restricted to more fleeting interactions. At least, Kiesler and Corbin found a different relationship between attraction and influence when the subject did not expect a fleeting interaction.

In a sense, if another does not like us and we do not expect any future interaction with him, then we say the devil take him and go our separate ways. If, however, we do expect future interaction, then somehow we have to deal with disagreements that arise between ourselves and the unattractive other. Other data (e.g., Darley and Berscheid, 1967; Kiesler, Kiesler, and Pallak, 1967) show that commitment to future interaction affects how we *do* react to particular situations, partly because it affects how we *can* react in these situations. Commitment affects both attitudinal and strategic factors in interpersonal relationships. It should guide not only resolution of interpersonal disagreement but also our general approach to group and interpersonal interaction by limiting the responses we can make to interactions with others. (Recall the Kiesler, Kiesler, and Pallak study, which shows how commitment to future interaction affects our reactions to a *faux pas* of another and determines whether or not we attempt to correct such norm violations.) In sum, one must be careful to determine whether a particular empirical statement is limited to a fleeting interaction or whether it could also be expected to occur in a long-term or more stable interaction.

Commitment to future interaction is conceptually related to two other theoretical constructs of interest. These are cohesiveness, which we discussed briefly before, and the comparison level for alternatives, which we have not previously mentioned (Thibaut and Kelley, 1959). The specifics of the relationship between these two variables and commitment to future interaction are not yet clear. Recall that we defined cohesiveness as the net result of all forces acting on the individual to remain in the group. In that sense, commitment to future interaction should contribute dramatically to cohesiveness. However, merely to say that the commitment to future interaction contributes to cohesiveness obviously does not explain the empirical picture. If the anticipation of future interaction merely increases cohesiveness, then it should have increased private acceptance in the Kiesler and Corbin experiment, regardless of the level of attraction. Of course, Kiesler and Corbin did not find a simple elevation of influence, but rather that the effect of commitment to future interaction was concentrated in the low-attraction condition. Thus, a theoretical statement that commitment to future interaction merely contributes to cohesiveness does not seem to be an adequate description of the data.

The relationship of commitment to future interaction to the concept called "comparison level for alternatives" is clearer. Again, however, this concept does not seem to explain all the data. The comparison level for alternatives simply says that how we evaluate a particular thing in our psychological field depends on what other things are open to us. We evaluate a particular object more positively if all the other objects available to us are even less positive. To direct the concept of comparison level for alternatives towards an explanation of the Kiesler and Corbin data, however, requires that the comparison level of alternatives be effective or salient only under certain conditions (e.g., low attraction). Otherwise, of course, we would be led to a prediction similar to cohesiveness, that commitment to future interaction would merely elevate private acceptance regardless of the level of attraction. It is likely that these data on the effect of commitment to future interaction will ultimately lead to theoretical refinements in both the concepts of cohesiveness and of comparison level for alternatives.

Sanctions and Surveillance.

Sanctions refer to the penalties that a group has at its disposal to enforce compliance. Surveillance refers to the degree to which the group may observe the individual in situations in which the behavioral or attitudinal norm is supposed to be displayed. Sanctions and surveillance underlie the enforcement of group norms. Obviously, groups do indeed enforce norms, whether the group is a criminal gang (Thrasher, 1927), a "street-corner society" (Whyte, 1943), or groups in experimental settings (Schachter, 1951). It should also be obvious that stiff sanctions and close surveillance determine the degree of compliance with group norms. However, we would like to add here that the overt nature of sanctions does not affect only overt behavior (as, say, French and Raven suggest), but sometimes can also affect the acceptance of the group's norms relative to the behavior. That is, if a person disagrees with the group and the group can observe his relevant behavior and punish his deviations, French and Raven imply that the correct behavior will be performed but not internalized.* Is it always true that behavior under extreme sanctions is not internalized? Perhaps not.

Sometimes, the overt nature of sanctions produces pressures upon the person to re-evaluate his beliefs, irrelevant to the power of the other or the degree of dissonance produced by the behavior. That is, the group's use of extreme sanctions to enforce a norm may have an additional implication for the individual. From the use of heavy sanctions, he might infer that this particular piece of behavior is very important to the group, perhaps central to its meaning. Such an inference would lead the individual to reassess his own opinions in that light, and as a result perhaps change his opinions. We are merely noting here that the effect of extreme sanctions and surveillance upon private acceptance may not be as simple as one would otherwise be led to believe.

However, the use of sanctions and surveillance can create other problems for the group. One study (Strickland, 1958) suggests this quite clearly. In that study, subjects played the role of supervisors and a confederate played the role of an underling. The degree of surveillance that the subject could have over the confederate's behavior was experimentally varied. When confederates were under the surveillance of subjects, subjects

---

*As we shall discuss in the next chapter, dissonance theory (Festinger, 1957) makes a similar prediction: private acceptance in such a situation would be inversely related to the degree of pressure for compliance.

perceived their behavior as being less internally derived than when the confederates were not under their surveillance. Thus, when a group maintains surveillance over its group members in order to ensure behavioral compliance, they may view the group members as less trustworthy and be less confident of the group member's true feelings about the group's norms.

Summary

In this chapter we have discussed the effect of one's relationship to the group upon private acceptance of group norms and opinions. We have emphasized individual factors, such as attraction to the individual group members, but have also noted some group factors, such as the interdependence among group members. Each type of variable contributes to the impact of the group on how the individual thinks and acts—the way he views his world.

However, knowledge about other people's opinions and behavior has an impact on us beyond our relationship to those individuals. The behavior and opinions of others, regardless of who they are, help to define social reality for us. This source of influence from the group may be referred to as a cognitive or informational source of influence, and we have alluded to it frequently in the present chapter. The cognitive impact of the group is the topic of the following chapter.

CHAPTER FIVE

Private Acceptance
and Cognitive Variables

In the previous chapter we discussed how one's relationship to others affects the private acceptance of influence from them. As mentioned, all intergroup influence does not stem from one's relation to the group—other variables also affect the acceptance of influence from others. We have labeled these extrarelational variables informational or cognitive sources of influence. The present chapter will concentrate on some of these.

What do we mean by cognitive sources of influence? To some extent, it is an arbitrary classification, not having great theoretical significance. To facilitate presentation, we have simply divided the set of possible sources of influence in group interaction into two subsets: those depending on one's relationship to the group, and those not. As with most subsets defined by the lack of a property (e.g., X and $not\text{-}X$), the variables discussed in the present chapter are rather heterogeneous. Most of these leftover variables have not been investigated thoroughly in a group setting. Indeed, investigators interested in group influence have largely ignored them. Their empirical and theoretical base has come from the study of individuals—how individuals categorize information they receive and when they accept it as valid. Since individuals exist largely as members of some group or another, we feel that such sources of influence are important for the study of group influence.

Let us take an example. In the last chapter we discussed the empirical generalization that the more attracted a person is to a group, the greater the influence the group may have on him. But why? One possible mediating factor (or intervening variable) is our expectation that information attractive others give us is more credible or trustworthy, and therefore we are more likely to believe it. That is what credible means—believable. But attractiveness and credibility are two variables, not one, and they should be experimentally and theoretically separated.

Does the effect of an attractive group depend solely on credibility as a mediating variable? That is, when there is no difference in credibility between conditions, will attractiveness still have an effect? There is no impeccable answer, but the question does suggest that a group psychologist should not ignore credibility as a source of influence in group interaction.

Indeed, credibility is precisely the type of variable this chapter concentrates upon. It is typical in four respects: it has not received much attention from group psychologists, it does not necessarily depend on any particular relationship of the individual to the group; it has been quite thoroughly investigated by "cognitive psychologists", i.e., those interested in the individual and how he receives and accepts information from the outside; and we feel it is important for the study of group influence.

The chapter is divided into three sections: variables affecting the acceptance of information from the group as valid, the effect of reinforcement coming from the group, and dissonance as a source of influence in a group setting (Festinger, 1957; see also Zimbardo and Ebbesen, to be published). The three topics are presented in that order.

WHEN DO WE BELIEVE WHAT OTHERS TELL US?

Credibility and Trustworthiness

To many questions or conflicts, people feel there is a correct answer, or even a correct opinion. No one can obtain firsthand all the information necessary to substantiate his many opinions. Any individual, no matter what his expertise in one area, must depend on others for second-hand, but hopefully expert, information in other areas. In obtaining this information, we tend to classify other people as more or less credible or trustworthy sources. The more credible the communicator, the more powerful his effect on us. Often a person who is expert in only one area is also able to influence people in areas in which he is not expert. Such data allow us to differentiate partially between expertise ("he should know") and trustworthiness ("he wouldn't lie to us"). The communicator may derive credibility from an area in which he is expert, and his credibility may carry over or generalize to situations in which he is not expert (e.g., an urban sociologist talking about international fiscal policy). A group that we have joined for one particular purpose (the Society for the Study of the Wizard of Oz) can influence us in other areas as well (should turtlenecks be worn with semiformal attire?). We learn to trust certain others as valid sources of information in particular areas. To a considerable extent, however, this trust or credibility generalizes to other areas not involved in the formation of the trust.

However, the tendency for a source's credibility in one area to generalize to another area is far from complete. For example, normally school teachers are credible sources for children. Nevertheless, Berenda (1950) found that school children conform much more on judgmental tasks to the judgments of their peers than to those of their teachers. There should be many topics on which school peers are considered to be more valid or correct sources of information than teachers, such as the value of sports activities, the correct length of one's hair, dating behavior, and general attire. If we want to influence someone, we might have to do some preliminary investigation to find out which communicators are considered to be credible for which particular topic. Given this, however, we could rest assured that the effects of a credible communicator would be powerful.

There is a possible exception to this, however. There is a class of opinions, of some indeterminate size, that the individual appears not to view as open to influence. On these attitudinal issues, the person apparently thinks that there is either no correct opinion, or that he is as entitled as anyone to his opinion. Such topics perhaps include a belief in God, attitudes towards classical music and modern art, politics (especially a preference for presidential candidate A over presidential candidate B), and to some extent attitudes towards minority groups. These attitudes are not yet well understood, but they may depend upon a conditioning of emotion in early childhood. At any rate, many of them appear to be relatively impervious to cognitive or informational sources of influence.

Relative Ability

Part of the impact of the group on the individual depends upon his belief that the group's judgment or norm is more likely to be correct than his own judgment or attitude. Two things in particular contribute to this belief: the self-confidence of the individual, and the previous history of success and failure of both the person and the group in this situation. The less confident the individual is in his opinion or judgment, the more the group may influence him. This is quite rational. Suppose a subject hears a number of clicks on a tape recorder and is asked to judge how many clicks there were. Suppose further that he felt there were about forty but the rest of the group uniformly thought that there were about seventy. Other things equal, the subject's ultimate judgment would depend on his confidence in his original opinion. If the clicks had sounded slowly and the individual had actually counted them, then the group would have minimal influence on him. However, if the clicks had come in quick succession, the individual would be less confident about his original judgment and be more likely to think the group accurate in its judgment.

Employing a click-counting task, League and Jackson (1964) found that subjects scoring low in self-esteem on a personality test conformed more closely to a bogus group judgment than did subjects who typically evaluated themselves more positively. The low self-esteem subjects were probably less confident of their estimates. Adding to this chronic lack of confidence, League and Jackson did find that low self-esteem subjects were actually less accurate in estimating the number of clicks. Apparently, their lack of confidence was justified (or maybe they justified their insecurity by not doing well).

Lack of confidence leads to a quite rational leaning upon others for the correct answers. A reduction in confidence need not stem from personality or ability factors (as in the League and Johnson study). If the group uniformly disagrees with the subject, his confidence in his own judgment will be shaken. In addition, the relative confidence of others affects their ability to influence us. We accept information from confident others, and their opinions have more influence than the opinions of those not so sure of themselves. Thus, disagreement with a group can shake one's confidence and induce him to accept the group's opinion as valid (although the disagreement may decrease the group's attractiveness).

The previous learning history of the individual may determine his confidence. Prior success of the group or prior failure of the subject on a given task enhances the subsequent conformity of the subject to the group norm. Obvious? Perhaps—but we expect an effect beyond the simple reward or punishment involved. Suppose a teenager's group has informal rules about proper attire for dates. Suppose further that the teenager does not adhere to these rules of dress on a date (e.g., a windbreaker instead of a jacket to a party). As a final variation in our little experiment, the girl laughs at him. From a very simple-minded notion of rewards and punishments, our subject should quit wearing windbreakers to parties. However, the norms of the group on dress have also proved successful, at least in that deviation resulted in punishment. Consequently, not only do we expect greater adherence to the group norm regarding jackets, but we also expect greater adherence to the group norms for other forms of dress as well. If adherence to the group's norms led to reward and helped to avoid punishment on a number of occasions, the person's attraction to the group might increase. Later we may test whether the group could influence this individual in an entirely different field, perhaps politics. If we found that they were able to influence him, would you say that this was due to the increased attractiveness of the group or the subject's view of the group as a valid source of information? Again, it is a question of separating the variables for precise explanation.

The Range of Possible Opinion

Ostrom and Upshaw (1968) asked subjects to play the role of a court judge. They gave them the history of a case up for trial and asked them to indicate how lenient they would be with the defendant. They then gave them another scale asking the subjects to how many years in prison they, as judge, would sentence the defendant. Ostrom and Upshaw varied the possible range of sentencing in this last questionnaire. For one subject, the questionnaire on sentencing might have a range from 1 year to 5 years. For another subject, the range might go from 1 year to 25 years. The question was, how did the subject's classification of himself as lenient or harsh affect his subsequent hypothetical sentencing of the defendant? Interestingly enough, it was found that the sentence depended upon both the subject's classification of himself on the leniency scale and the range of possible years of sentencing. In other words, a subject who classified himself as a moderately harsh judge might sentence the defendant to 4 years when presented with a possible scale of 1 to 5 years. On the other hand, another subject who also classified himself as moderately harsh would give 20 years on the 1 to 25 scale. The range of possible opinions on sentencing was crucial to the subject's actual behavior. If he classified himself as middle-of-the-road, then he was middle-of-the-road on whatever range of possible opinions presented to him, whether that range meant sentencing the defendant to 4 or to 20 years.

To some extent, this is a scaling or measurement problem. In another sense, these data suggest that the individual classifies himself in terms of the extremeness of his attitude (or how unusual he is) and then behaves with the same degree of extremeness within what he considers to be the range of possible behaviors. By the same token, the group might define a range of possible attitudes that an individual member could hold. Within this range of defined "reasonable attitudes" the individual might have a particular conception of himself. Say, one defines himself as a progressive fellow. What a "progressive fellow" does and believes when his reference group is The American Manufacturers' Association is quite different than when the "progressive fellow" belongs to the American Psychological Association. If we induce two businessmen, one a self-defined progressive and another a self-defined conservative, to become psychologists, we expect changes in their attitudes and opinions as a result. Each probably would become more liberal in his outlook. In addition, making a wild inference from the Ostrom and Upshaw data, it is possible that they still might be referring to themselves respectively as progressive and conservative with the same absolute difference between their respective new attitudes as between their old attitudes.

Information Restriction and the Need to Be Correct

We have discussed Festinger's social comparison theory in Chapter 3. That theory assumes that "individuals are motivated to be correct" in their opinions. However, in social reality (as opposed to physical reality) there is no impeccable way to be correct in one's opinions. Correctness is defined by others. The attitudes, opinions, and behavior of other people define social reality, including private attitudes and the private acceptance of influence from others. The groups to which we belong, formal or informal, give us information on what attitudes are correct.

We add here that not only does the group define the correct attitude, but it is also a primary source of information relevant to our attitudes. As mentioned, we seldom know all there is to know about a given issue. Our interactions with others provide us with information about attitudinal issues. For example, Katz and Lazarsfeld (1955) have referred to the two-step flow of communication. In inspecting the impact of magazine and newspaper articles, they discovered a particular channel of communication. They say that only a small number of people, whom they call opinion leaders, actually read and digest such information-laden articles. These opinion leaders, Katz and Lazarsfeld say, are the first step in the flow of communication, and they then become primary sources of information about these issues to others in their community, neighborhood, and groups. In sum, groups not only define a range of reasonable attitudes to hold for an individual, they also define the correct attitude to hold, and lastly they provide the very information by which the attitude is formed. It should come as no surprise to us that groups are very powerful sources of influence.

REINFORCEMENT

Reinforcement in a Group Setting

Bavelas, Hastorf, Gross, and Kite (1965) have recently shown that both the sociometric (liking) and communication patterns of a group can be altered by appropriate reinforcement of an individual member's verbal output in the group. In this experiment, subjects took part in four-man groups and discussed three human relations problems "so that the dynamics of the group discussion process could be analyzed." After each discussion period, the subjects completed a short sociometric questionnaire in which they were asked to rank all group members, including themselves, on four key items: the amount of participation in the discussion, the quality of ideas each member presented in the discussion, the effectiveness of each member in guiding the discussion, and general leadership ability. Thus far it sounds like a typical group communication experiment, but Bavelas *et al.* delivered various reinforcements for talking during the course of the second discussion.

The first discussion provided a baseline of verbal output for individual members. On the basis of this discussion, Bavelas *et al.* picked the man ranked third (i.e., next to last) for appropriate reinforcement. He was called the "target person." Subjects in certain conditions expected to be told how they were doing as the discussion proceeded by means of small red and green lights in front of them. Subjects were told, "Whenever you make a contribution to the discussion which is helpful or functional in facilitating the group process, your green light will go on . . . whenever you behave in a way that will eventually hamper or hinder the group process, your red light will go on . . . ." (Bavelas *et al.*, 1965, p. 58.) Subjects were also told that silence during the discussion could either contribute to or detract from the group process and that the green lights and red lights could flash during silent periods as well.

In the second group discussion, the experimenter tried to flash the target person's green light whenever he made declarative statements or stated an opinion, but tried to flash the three other members' red lights if they engaged in the same behavior. In addition, the other group members received green lights for interacting with the target person, and especially for agreeing with him. On occasion, the target person received a red light for remaining silent. These lights were used only in the second discussion. In the third group discussion, as in the first, groups were left on their own and no lights were used.

There were three separate dependent measures in this experiment: the sheer quantity of the individual's verbal output (how much he said), sociometric ranking (quality of ideas, etc.) given him by other group members, and the person's ranking of himself. The lights were used only in the second session, so we may appropriately inspect the difference in these scores between the first and second sessions to test the effect of the lights, and the difference between the first and third sessions to see if the effect of the lights persisted. Results were as expected. The target subjects increased their verbal output from the first session to the second session. On the sociometric indices, these individuals not only rated their own performance of better quality than in the first session, but the other group members also considered his performance to be better. In the third discussion period, when lights were not used, all of these indices decreased somewhat but they were still significantly better than in the first session.

Thus, the experimenter's positive and negative evaluations of the quality of the contribution in the group setting not only immediately affected the individual's behavior and the others' reactions to it, but these effects were maintained in a third session in which the reinforcing cues were no longer present. Bavelas *et al.* designed several other conditions to look for the underlying parameters of the effect. For example, they found that the effect was not due to the judgment of the experimenter about what to reinforce—the effect was also obtained with a preprogrammed unit connected to a multiple-position stepping switch. This switch moved in coordination with a recording of each discrete utterance by any of the subjects. In this manner, each subject could have a preprogrammed fixed sequence of lights. The encouragement of the target person's talking and the discouragement of the others' talking was programmed in advance. The effects still occurred. However, they did not hold for any of the following conditions: when the reinforcement was given randomly, when only the target person was reinforced but not the others in the group, and when the target person was not reinforced but the others in the group were discouraged from talking. This may mean that the main results were not due to the reinforcement schedules *per se*. First we have to get the target person to talk, but we also have to reinforce the others for agreeing with him.

What relevance do these data have for private acceptance? The experiment did show how one's performance in a group setting could be altered by external reinforcement. What we are suggesting is that the result of the reinforcement—one's performance in the group setting—mediates other effects related to private acceptance. Although Bavelas *et al.* did not present data on this point, it is quite likely that the target person's attraction to the group was increased by their procedure. (They did find that the target person liked the critical discussion problem better than the other problems.) Increased attraction to the group, if it did indeed occur, could mediate subsequent influence attempts of the group for the individual. It also might make him feel more committed to the group. We do know that the other group members evaluated the target person more highly (quality of ideas, leadership ability, and so forth). We should certainly expect that, as a result of relatively heightened value, the target person should have greater influence over other group members. Although this issue is completely unresearched, the Bavelas technique for altering group structure could lead to a substantial contributuion in the study of interpersonal influence and its antecedent conditions.

The Reinforcement of Repeated Behaviors under Surveillance

We have said before that, while a group may enforce its norms by resorting to extreme pressure, extreme pressure is likely to produce compliance but not private acceptance. To ensure continued behavioral adherence, the group must keep the individual member under surveillance. Surveillance is costly, time-consuming, and possibly distasteful. The question we will briefly approach here is how one could produce private acceptance without continued surveillance.

Although it has never been investigated, we suggest the following as a technique. To begin, one produces the behavior by pressure and continues it by surveillance. However, one arranges for periodic reinforcement of the behavior, even though surveillance is continued. Subsequently, one can test for the occurrence of the behavior when there is no surveillance. Indeed, the Chinese methods of dealing with U.S. prisoners of war in Korea suggest that constant surveillance is probably not a good technique. Prisoners knew informers existed, but not who and how many. Their captors would often confront them with minor deviations from rules, as if to illustrate that they knew everything that went on in the compound (Schein, 1958). To produce good results, perhaps the subject should know explicitly that surveillance is not constant, but at the same time not know when he is under surveillance.

If the subject continues to perform the behavior, and he knows that he is not consistently under surveillance, then his behavior appears to him to be more "self-emitted." If we then arrange for his new behavior to be occasionally reinforced (perhaps not from the group members), then we may have the conditions for a more permanent behavioral change and a consequent private acceptance of the group norm.

This sounds very mechanistic and Orwellian—but we are convinced that, to some extent at least, this is what parents unwittingly do to teach their children certain rules of society. Parents seem to tune children in and out, even in close physical proximity. A transgression missed at one time might be attended to if repeated later. From the child's point of view, it is inconsistent surveillance. The pressure for compliance with social or family rules also varies, depending largely on the parent's mood or the frequency of previous transgressions.

There are also other data and theories on the relationship of behavior and surveillance to private acceptance. These are more appropriately discussed later in the chapter under the heading of dissonance theory.

The perception of one's own behavior. Bem (1965) has argued that one's own behavior determines one's attitudes. He says that attitudes are not as well structured, well formed, and self-recognized as theorists and experimenters would have us believe. According to Bem, our attitudes are determined by our previous behavior and whether we think the behavior was self-determined. If a person were asked, "Do you like brown bread?", then Bem's hypothetical subject might answer, "I guess so, I'm always eating it." However, one's interpretation of the behavior also depends upon whether one perceives that behavior as being "self-emitted." Therefore, the subject could alternatively say, "I don't know if I like brown bread, my mother always made me eat it."

Bem's model has not received much direct experimental attention. However, Kiesler, Zanna, and Nisbett (1968) suggested a revision of the theory and tested it. They suggested that for one to infer an attitude from his behavior, it is necessary to have an attitude that is not well formed, a behavior that is not very discrepant from this attitude, and some implication that the behavior is relevant to the attitude. They tested this hypothesis by asking subjects to perform some specific behavior that was either fairly consistent or discrepant with their previous vague attitude. Independently of this, the behavior was suggested to be either relevant or irrelevant to their attitude. They found that only under the conditions when the subject's behavior was not too discrepant with his attitude, and when he believed it relevant to his attitude, did he define his attitude on the basis of the behavior. Subjects were asked to convince people on the streets that either something should be done about air pollution or nothing should be done about it. Prior to the experiment, subjects generally believed that something should be done. They agreed to perform the behavior under a condition of either belief-irrelevance (the experimenter said he chose the topic for scientific reasons) or belief-relevance (the experimenter said he chose the topic because he believed in the issue). Only when the subject was behaving consistently with his beliefs *and* the behavior was made relevant to his belief did he become more favorable to action on air pollution.

When a person does not have a well-formed attitude and perhaps not much information about the issue, he will use his previous behavior to infer his own attitude. Under these conditions, the person appears to be saying something like the following to himself: "What do I really think about this issue or norm? Well, I really don't know, let me see . . . Well, I did *X*, so I guess I believe *X*." It might be that such a process of inference of one's attitude or belief on the basis of prior behavior is especially prevalent in children. On the basis of the Kiesler, Zanna, and Nisbett data, it appears that this process occurs only when the behavior is not inconsistent with one's prior belief. In the discussion to follow, on dissonance theory, we shall show what happens when one behaves inconsistently with his beliefs.

DISSONANCE THEORY AND RELATED EFFECTS

Dissonance Theory

The primary input for dissonance theory is something that Festinger calls cognitions (Festinger, 1957, 1964; Brehm and Cohen, 1962; see also Zimbardo and Ebbesen, to be published, for a more detailed discussion). Cognitions are bits of information about oneself and one's world. Examples of them could be: "I smoke cigarettes." "My lawn is green." "I am a Democrat." "I believe that people should not lie." "I am attracted to this group." The theory is concerned primarily with relationships among these cognitions. Any pair of cognitions presumably has one of three relationships. The cognitive elements in the pair can be: inconsistent, consistent, or irrelevant. These relationships are defined in terms of the psychological implications of one cognitive element for another. If one cognitive element would tend to imply the opposite of the other cognitive element, then these two cognitions are in a dissonant relationship. If one cognition implies the other cognition, then they are said to be in a consonant relationship. If there is no necessary implication between the two members of the cognitive pair, then the relationship is said to be irrelevant. Thus, the two cognitions "I smoke heavily" and "smoking causes cancer" are dissonant. The two cognitions "I am a good father" and "I took my son to the circus" are probably in a consonant relationship; whereas the two cognitions "the grass on my lawn is green" and "water is boiling on the stove" are irrelevant to one another. One can see that the relationship between two cognitions depends on the psychological implication of one cognition for another, not on the logical implication. The two cognitions above—being a father and taking one's son to the circus—might be dissonant in one culture but not in another. Indeed, they might be dissonant for one person in a given culture, but not for another person. In a sense, it depends on the subject's perception of his psychological world—what he perceives to fit together.

Theoretically, when two cognitions are in an inconsistent relationship, dissonance is produced. Dissonance is an uncomfortable state and the person is motivated to reduce it. The more dissonance a person has, then theoretically the greater the pressure upon him to reduce it. The amount of dissonance is determined by both the degree to which two cognitions are inconsistent and the importance of the cognitions for the subject.

How can dissonance be reduced? Festinger (1957) mentions three ways. First, the subject could change a cognition related to his behavior. With the two cognitions "I smoke heavily" and "smoking causes cancer" our subject is in a state of psychological dissonance. However, he could reduce this dissonance very simply by quitting smoking—a behavioral change. A second method of reducing dissonance is to change a cognition relating to one's physical or psychological environment. Thus, if dissonance is produced between the two cognitions "I am a person of prestige and wealth" and "I work in a dilapidated office," then the suggested or implied change in one's environment is quite clear.

A third way of reducing dissonance is to add an element or elements to the relationship. Suppose dissonance is aroused by joining a group which one subsequently finds is dull and boring. One way to reduce this dissonance is to seek out other aspects of the group which would justify membership (remember our discussion of functional autonomy of motives?). Some psychological distortion, such as artificially enhancing the prestige of the group, would reduce the dissonance (although some dissonance would probably remain).

What are the implications of dissonance theory for group behavior and conformity? We will restrict ourselves to two illustrations by appropriate experimental examples. Group initiation provides the first example (Aronson and Mills, 1959). The second example illustrates how private acceptance may be affected by public compliance to a discrepant group norm (Kiesler and De Salvo, 1967).

Aronson and Mills were interested in the effect of severity of initiation on liking for a group. Suppose a person has undergone an unpleasant experience to become a member of a group, and then finds that the group is not particularly attractive. "If a person has undergone an unpleasant initiation to gain an admission to the group, his cognition that he has gone through an unpleasant experience for the sake of group membership is dissonant with his cognition that there are things about the group that he does not like. He can reduce this dissonance in two ways. He can convince himself that the initiation was not very unpleasant, or he can exaggerate the positive characteristics of the group and minimize its negative aspects. With increasing severity of initiation, it becomes more and more difficult to believe that the initiation was not very bad. Thus, a person who has gone through a painful initiation to become a member of a group should tend to reduce his dissonance by overestimating the attractiveness of the group." (Aronson and Mills, 1959, p. 178.) They hypothesized, then, that the more severe the initiation for gaining membership into a group, the greater the dissonance. The person should reduce the dissonance by distorting the attractiveness of the group. Consequently, the person who has undergone a severe initiation should subsequently evaluate the group more positively than the person who has undergone a mild initiation.

College girls volunteered as subjects to participate in a discussion group on sex. They were randomly assigned to one of three conditions. One condition entailed a severe initiation, one a mild initiation, and one was a control condition. All subjects were told that they were joining an ongoing group to replace a girl who had dropped out. They were also told that the experimenter was interested in the group discussion process and wanted people to participate who would not be embarrassed by the discussion of sex. In the control condition, subjects were merely asked if they thought they could discuss sex freely. If they indicated that they could, they were admitted as members of the group. In the experimental conditions, the experimenter said that the subject would have to go through an "embarrassment test" before she could be admitted to the group. In the severe condition, the subjects first read aloud, as part of this test, twelve obscene words listed on cards, and then read aloud (in front of the male experimenter) two descriptions of rather explicit sexual activity from contemporary novels. In the mild initiation condition, the subjects merely read a number of words that were related to sex but were certainly not obscene. After subjects in both the mild and severe conditions had finished their material, they were told that they were admitted to the group.

All subjects were then told that the group was presently in session but that, since the new member had not read the material assigned for that day, she would not be allowed to take part. However, the subject was allowed to listen to the discussion and promised that she could participate in the next meeting. Each girl then put on earphones and listened to a group discussion. All actually heard the same bogus interaction. The group discussion was ". . . .deliberately designed to be as dull and banal as possible in order to maximize the dissonance of the subjects in the severe condition. The participants spoke drily and haltingly on secondary sex behavior in the lower animals, 'inadvertently' contradicted themselves and one another, mumbled several *non sequiturs,* started sentences that they never finished, hemmed, hawed, and in general conducted one of the most worthless and uninteresting discussions imaginable." (Aronson and Mills, 1959, p. 179.)

Afterwards, the experimenter explained that all the people participating filled out several scales at the end of each session. He asked the subject to fill out these scales as well. Nine of the scales concerned reactions to the discussion, and eight were related to the subject's evaluation of the group participants. The results from these ratings are presented in Table 5-1. The results of both the evaluation of the discussion and the evaluation of the participants were similar. The control subjects and the subjects who underwent the mild initiation evaluated the discussion and the participants at about the same level. However, the subjects who underwent the severe initiation evaluated both the discussion and the participants much more positively than either those who underwent the mild initiation or the control subjects.

TABLE 5-1

The Effect of Severity of Initiation on Liking for a Group: Means of the Sum of Ratings for the Different Experimental Conditions (from Aronson and Mills, 1959)

	Experimental Conditions		
Rating Scales	Control (N = 21)	Mild (N = 21)	Severe (N = 21)
Discussion (9) Mean	80.2	81.8	97.6
Participants (8) Mean	89.9	89.3	97.7

Theoretically, the severe initiation produced dissonance. The dissonance was between the cognitions "I underwent a difficult and embarrassing task in order to join this group" and "the group is dull and banal." To reduce this dissonance, the subjects apparently distorted and enhanced the attractiveness of both the other members of the group and the quality of their discussion. (See Gerard and Mathewson, 1966, for a nice replication of this experiment in which shock was substituted for the sexual material in the initiation procedure.) One would expect these results to generalize to other aspects of behavior in a group interaction. For example, suppose a person belonged to a mildly interesting political discussion group. Suppose, further, that the group induced her to become politically involved, distributing leaflets and the like. If the behavior was effortful and not justified by the person's initial attraction to the group, dissonance would be produced. If the behavior were extremely effortful (so that one could not distort the amount of effort that went into it), then the dissonance could best be reduced by the person distorting the group's attractiveness. In turn, enhanced attractiveness of the group could mediate subsequent influence of the individual by the group. Let us now turn to the second experiment for discussion.

Kiesler and De Salvo (1967) were interested in the interactive effects of the attractiveness of the group, and the subject's compliance with the group's wishes, upon subsequent private acceptance of the norm. In their experiment, each subject thought she disagreed with the group about which of two tasks the group was to work on. Two theoretically relevant variables were manipulated in this experiment. First, two levels of attraction to the group were obtained using a bogus measure of attraction to others. In each experimental group of four college girls, two subjects thought they would like the group very much and two subjects were led to believe that they would not like the group very much. This constituted the attractiveness manipulation. Independently of this, half of the subjects were induced to go along with the group—to comply with the group's wishes (the compliance condition). The other half of the subjects knew only that the group disagreed with them (the preference condition). They knew only that the group preferred task *B* over task *A*. They were not asked to go along with the group and indeed they did not know which task the group was actually going to work on.

What effect would we expect attraction to have when the group had only stated a preference? This should be quite clear. According to data we have discussed before, the more attractive group should influence the subject more than would the less attractive group. In the preference condition, the greater the manipulated attraction, the greater should be the change in the subject's opinions (about the two tasks) towards the opinion of the group.

In the compliance condition, the subject was induced to go along with the group choice. In this condition, "the experimenter stated that if anyone disagreed with the group choice, she was free to leave. However, he emphasized that if someone left, the rest of the group would have to work somewhat longer. The latter sentence was added to ensure that the pressure for compliance would be perceived as emanating from the group rather than from the experimenter. The experimenter asked everyone willing to work on the 'group choice' to raise her hand. In every group, everyone raised her hand. Thus, in the compliance condition, subjects publicly complied with the group's choice of task, even though they disagreed with the group about this choice." (Kiesler and De Salvo, 1967, p. 163.)

What effect would you expect attraction to have in this compliance condition? Perhaps you are correct. In the compliance condition, Kiesler and De Salvo analyzed the situation according to dissonance theory. This subject had not just stated a preference, she had actually performed some behavior—she had agreed to go along with the group. She was induced by the group to work on a task that she did not prefer. In this situation, Kiesler and De Salvo reasoned, the less attractive the group, the greater the dissonance produced by the decision to go along with the group. The dissonance is between the cognition "I do not like this group very much" and the cognition "I have acceded to their wish to work on the dull task."

To reduce the dissonance, then, the subject should re-evaluate the task accordingly. She should enhance the attractiveness of the task that the group induced her to work on, and derogate the attractiveness of the task that she had formerly preferred. A sum of these two measures (a measure of dissonance reduction) was the dependent variable.

The effect of attraction on private acceptance of the task preferred by the group should be entirely dependent on whether the group induced the subject to go along with their wishes or whether the group had merely stated a preference. These data are presented in Table 5-2 and, as one can see, they are in line with expectations. When the group had only stated a preference, the more attractive the group, then the greater the change in the subject's perception of the two tasks. However, under the compliance condition, the effects were reversed. When the subject was induced to go along with the group, then the less attractive the group, the greater the private acceptance of the group task.

TABLE 5-2

The Group as an Influencing Agent: Relative Dissonance Reduction in Four Experimental Conditions (from Kiesler and De Salvo, 1967)

Were subjects induced to comply with the group?	Attractiveness of the Group	
	High	Low
Compliance Total dissonance reduction	4.48 (N = 21)	13.56 (N = 23)
Preference Total dissonance reduction	12.69 (N = 19)	−.76 (N = 21)

The Kiesler and De Salvo experiment illustrates the complexity of group phenomena and shows how behavioral compliance with group norms is an important consideration for subsequent private acceptance of those norms. Compliance was experimentally controlled. If compliance were allowed to vary, then it would be affected by attraction: the more attractive the group, the more likely the subject would comply with the discrepant group norm, as discussed in Chapter 3. However, the Kiesler and De Salvo experiment shows that subjects highly attracted to the group would probably not privately accept the group norm, even though they might be more likely to comply with it. On the other hand, in an uncontrolled setting, the few unattracted subjects complying with the group norm would be dramatically affected in their private acceptance of the norm. Without control over compliance, attraction would work in two different directions at once within a group. On the one hand, high attraction would increase the percentage of subjects complying; on the other hand, it would reduce private acceptance.

Dissonance theory makes similar predictions in the group setting for variables other than attraction, as well. Theoretically, any cognition inconsistent with choosing the dull task would produce dissonance. Variables such as perceived volition in choosing the task, justification for choosing the task, or incentive for choosing the task should produce the same effects as those obtained by Kiesler and De Salvo. These variables mentioned have already been used in experiments where the agent inducing behavioral compliance is a single individual. The Kiesler and De Salvo experiment merely extends the dissonance paradigm to group effects—when a group induces the individual to comply with group norms.

The general dissonance hypothesis underlying the Kiesler and De Salvo experiment may be stated as follows: when an individual is induced to perform some behavior inconsistent with his beliefs, and the less the pressure put upon him to perform that behavior, then the greater the consequent attitude change towards consistency with the behavior. Greater pressure may be operationalized as greater attraction to the group, greater choice or volition in performing the behavior, greater justification for performing the behavior, and so forth. In all cases, we expect extreme pressure to comply to have little effect upon private acceptance. Sometimes, people even react negatively to extreme pressure and change their attitudes in the opposite direction. This is discussed below under Brehm's reactance theory.

Reactance

Brehm (1966) argues that people like to feel that they have control over their behavior and that they are free to behave as they wish. Brehm says that this feeling of "behavioral freedom" is very important to the individual and that if this freedom is reduced or threatened, the individual will become motivationally aroused. This motivation Brehm calls "psychological reactance." When reactance is aroused, the person not only tries to prevent further loss of behavioral freedom, but also tries to re-establish the lost freedom. Brehm has conducted a number of experiments on reactance, but we will limit ourselves to one illustration.

This experiment concerns the effects of one person performing a favor for another. Brehm says that usually a favor enhances one's impression of the person who performs it and also obligates one to return it. When it is not important for the person to be free of obligation to another, then a favor should arouse little reactance. However, Brehm says, when it is relatively important to be free of obligation to another, then a favor should arouse reactance and a consequent tendency to avoid doing a return favor. Brehm and Cole (1966) tested this notion in a very clever experiment.

When subjects reported for the experiment, they found a note on the door of the experimental room asking them to wait in a chair there. A confederate showed up, read the note, and also took a chair. The experimenter then appeared and announced there would be a short wait until the experimental materials were prepared. The confederate asked if he could leave for a few minutes and the experimenter agreed. While the confederate was gone, the experimenter engaged the subject in casual conversation and then tried to make it more or less important for the subject to be free of obligation to the confederate. In the high-importance condition, she told subjects that impression ratings they were going to make subsequently in the experiment were the beginnings of a large research project and that it was very important for the subject to be as careful and accurate in these ratings as he could. In the low-importance condition, subjects were told that the ratings were for a sociological student research project and therefore not of much consequence.

Later, the confederate returned and did one of two things. In the no-favor condition, he simply took the chair without comment. In the favor condition, he gave the subject a soft drink and refused payment if any were offered. The experimenter quickly invited the two into the experimental room. Subsequently, the subject and the confederate filled out various forms rating each's first impression of the other. When these were completed, the experimenter placed a stack of papers in front of the confederate and asked him to sort them into various piles. The dependent variable was whether the subject would help the confederate, i.e., whether he would return the previous favor of a soft drink.

Without a previous favor, about half of the subjects helped the confederate, regardless of the importance manipulation. When a favor had been performed (i.e., when the confederate had brought a soft drink for the subject), then in the low-importance condition, fourteen of the fifteen subjects volunteered to help the confederate. This was as expected. When it is not important to be free of obligation to the other, the favor should not arouse reactance. However, Brehm and Cole theorized that when the subject's evaluation of the confederate is important, the favor should arouse reactance. It is important to be free, but freedom is threatened. The person reasserts his freedom by acting as if there were no obligation, and indeed overdoes it. Reactance should decrease the frequency of subjects volunteering to help the confederate in the paper-stacking task. The data supported the hypothesis. In the high-importance condition, only two of the fifteen subjects volunteered to help the confederate stack the papers.

Brehm's theory seems to be substantiated by this experiment, and his hypothesis should be applicable to group settings in a number of ways. For example, when a group puts extreme pressure on an individual to comply with some norm, perhaps this pressure would also threaten the individual's perceived freedom of behavior and arouse reactance. If so, then the person should attempt to resolve this reactance by acting in a manner contrary to the group. This is a problem worth working on. Similar effects have been noted in children's reactions to parental demands; e.g., intentionally botching a piano recital when performing at the parents' insistence in front of relatives, "not hearing" requests to do chores, and occasionally fighting when one has explicitly been told not to.

Summary

In this chapter, we have tried to explore various cognitive and informational sources of influence on private acceptance. Why use both terms "cognitive" and "informational" as sources of influence? Why not merely "informational" as perhaps was implied in Chapter 2? We feel the term "cognitive" is the broader term and adds something. "Informational" would certainly apply to such variables as credibility, where the acceptance of some particular information is the primary dependent variable. However, it is difficult to point to particular information accepted when discussing reinforcement or dissonance. Consequently, we use the term "cognitive" to describe all of the effects discussed in this chapter, and the term "informational" to refer only to the variables discussed in the first section of the chapter.

What we mentioned in the beginning of this chapter should now be obvious to the reader: these types of influence in group interaction have not been exhaustively investigated. We know they are important as sources of influence, but the primary investigations on these topics have not taken place in group interactions. The variables listed under our first section (credibility, etc.) have received a great deal of experimental attention, but mostly in communication settings where a large batch of subjects either read a communication or someone delivers it to them all at once. There is no real group involved. In our second section, reinforcement, we indicated that very little attention has been given to reinforcement in any part of social psychology, let alone group interaction. There, we tried to indicate some possibilities for research, some probable conclusions that one might draw, and some implications of current theory. In our third section, dissonance theory and its related effects, there has been a great deal of research. Once again, however, very little of this research has taken place in a group setting. It is unfortunate that the theory and data mentioned in this chapter abound in social psychology, but have yet been little attended to by group psychologists.

References

References

Allport, F. H., *Social psychology*. Boston: Houghton Mifflin, 1924.

Allport, F. H., A structuronomic conception of behavior: Individual and collective I. Structural theory and the master problem of social psychology. *Journal of Abnormal and Social Psychology*, 1962, **64**, 3-30.

Allport, G. W., *Personality: a psychological interpretation*. New York: Holt, 1937.

Aronson, E., and Mills, J., The effects of severity of initiation on liking for a group. *Journal of Abnormal and Social Psychology*, 1959, **59**, 177-181.

Asch, S. E., *Social psychology*. Englewood Cliffs, N.J.: Prentice Hall, 1952.

Asch, S. E., Effects of group pressures upon modification and distortion of judgments. In E. E. Maccoby, T. M. Newcomb, and E. L. Hartley (Eds.), *Readings in social psychology*. New York: Holt, 3rd edition, 1958, pp. 174-183.

Back, K. W., Influence through social communication. *Journal of Abnormal and Social Psychology*, 1951, **46**, 9-23.

Bandura, A., Vicarious processes: A case of no-trial learning. In L. Berkowitz (Ed.), *Advances in experimental social psychology*. Vol. 2. New York: Academic Press, 1965, pp. 3-57.

Bavelas, A., Hastorf, A. H., Gross, A. E., and Kite, W. R., Experiments on the alteration of group structure. *Journal of Experimental Social Psychology*, 1965, **1**, 55-70

Bem, D. J., An experimental analysis of self-persuasion. *Journal of Experimental Social Psychology*, 1965, **1**, 199-218.

Berenda, R. W., *The influence of the group on judgments of children*. New York: King's Crown Press, 1950.

Brehm, J. W., *A theory of psychological reactance.* New York: Academic Press, 1966.

Brehm, J. W., and Cohen, A. R., *Explorations in cognitive dissonance.* New York: Wiley, 1962.

Brehm, J. W., and Cole, A., Effect of a favor which reduces freedom. *Journal of Personality and Social Psychology,* 1966, **3**, 420-426.

Brown, R., *Social psychology.* New York: Free Press, 1965.

Byrne, D., Interpersonal attraction and attitude similarity. *Journal of Abnormal and Social Psychology,* 1961, **62**, 713-715.

Cantril, H., The invasion from Mars. In E. E. Maccoby, T. M. Newcomb, and E. L. Hartley (Eds.), *Readings in social psychology.* New York: Holt, 3rd edition, 1958, pp. 291-299.

Cartwright, D., and Zander, A. (Eds.), *Group dynamics.* Evanston, Illinois: Row and Peterson, 2nd edition, 1960.

Cartwright, D., and Zander, A., *Group dynamics.* New York: Harper and Row, 3rd edition, 1968.

Centers, R., *The psychology of social classes.* Princeton, N.J.: Princeton University Press, 1949.

Charters, W. W., Jr., and Newcomb, T. M., Some attitudinal effects of experimentally increased salience of a membership group. In E. E. Maccoby, T. M. Newcomb, and E. L. Hartley (Eds.), *Readings in social psychology.* New York: Holt, 3rd edition, 1958, pp. 276-280.

Clark, K. B., and Clark, M. P., Racial identification and preference in Negro children. In E. E. Maccoby, T. M. Newcomb, and E. L. Hartley (Eds.), *Readings in social psychology.* New York: Holt, 3rd edition, 1958, pp. 602-611.

Coch, L., and French, J. R. P., Jr., Overcoming resistance to change. *Human Relations,* 1948, **1**, 512-532.

Cohen, A. R., Upward communication in experimentally created hierarchies. *Human Relations,* 1958, **11**, 41-53.

Converse, P., and Campbell, A., Political standards in secondary groups. In D. Cartwright and A. Zander, *Group dynamics.* New York: Harper and Row, 3rd edition, 1968, pp. 199-214.

Darley, J. M., and Berscheid, E., Increased liking as a result of the anticipation of personal contact. *Human Relations,* 1967, **20**, 29-40.

Deutsch, M., An experimental study of the effects of cooperation and competition upon group process. *Human Relations,* 1949, **2**, 199-231.

Deutsch, M., Some factors affecting membership motivation and achievement motivation. *Human Relations,* 1959, **12**, 81-95.

Deutsch, M., and Gerard, H., A study of normative and informational social influences on individual judgment. *Journal of Abnormal and Social Psychology,* 1955, **51**, 629-636.

Douvan, E., Social status and success strivings. *Journal of Abnormal and Social Psychology*, 1956, **52**, 219-223.

Festinger, L., An analysis of compliant behavior. In M. Sherif and M. O. Wilson (Eds.), *Group relations at the crossroads*. New York: Harper, 1953, pp. 232-256.

Festinger, L., A theory of social comparison processes. *Human Relations*, 1954, **7**, 117-140.

Festinger, L., *A theory of cognitive dissonance*. Stanford: Stanford University Press, 1957.

Festinger, L., *Conflict, decision, and dissonance*. Stanford: Stanford University Press, 1964.

Festinger, L., Pepitone, A., and Newcomb, T., Some consequences of deindividuation in a group. *Journal of Abnormal and Social Psychology*, 1952, **47**, 382-389.

Festinger, L., Riecken, H. W., and Schachter, S., *When prophecy fails*. Minneapolis: University of Minnesota Press, 1956.

Festinger, L., Schachter, S., and Back, K., *Social pressures in informal groups: a study of human factors in housing*. New York: Harper, 1950.

Freedman, J. L., and Fraser, S. C., Compliance without pressure: the foot-in-the-door technique. *Journal of Personality and Social Psychology*, 1966, **4**, 195-202.

Freedman, J. L., Wallington, S. A., and Bless, E., Compliance without pressure: the effect of guilt. *Journal of Personality and Social Psychology*, 1967, **7**, 117-124.

French, J. R. P., Jr., and Raven, B. H., The bases of social power. In D. Cartwright (Ed.), *Studies in social power*. Ann Arbor: Institute for Social Research, 1959, pp. 150-167.

Gerard, H. B., The anchorage of opinions in face-to-face groups. *Human Relations*, 1954, **7**, 313-325.

Gerard, H. B., Deviation, conformity, and commitment. In I. D. Steiner and M. Fishbein (Eds.), *Current studies in social psychology*. New York: Holt, Rinehart, and Winston, 1965, pp. 263-276.

Gerard, H. B., and Mathewson, G. C., The effects of severity of initiation on liking for a group: a replication. *Journal of Experimental Social Psychology*, 1966, **2**, 278-287.

Golembiewski, R. T., *The small group: an analysis of research concepts and operations*. Chicago: University of Chicago Press, 1962.

Grinker, R., and Spiegel, J., *Men under stress*. Philadelphia: Blakiston, 1945.

Gross, N., McEachern, A. W., and Mason, W. S., Role conflict and its resolution. In E. E. Maccoby, T. M. Newcomb, and E. L. Hartley (Eds.), *Readings in social psychology*. New York: Holt, 3rd edition, 1958, pp. 447-458.

Hamblin, R. L., Leadership and crisis. *Sociometry*, 1958, **21**, 322-335.

Hare, A. P., *Handbook of small group research*. New York: Free Press, 1962.

Heider, F., *The psychology of interpersonal relations*. New York: Wiley, 1958.

Hollander, E. P., Conformity, status, and idiosyncrasy credit. *Psychological Review* 1958, **65**, 117-127.

Hollander, E. P., and Willis, R. H., Some current issues in the psychology of conformity and nonconformity. *Psychological Bulletin,* 1967, **68**, 62-76.

Homans, G. C., *The human group*. New York: Harcourt, Brace, 1950.

Jacobs, R. C., and Campbell, D. T., The perpetuation of an arbitrary tradition through several generations of a laboratory microculture. *Journal of Abnormal and Social Psychology,* 1961, **62**, 649-658.

Jones, E. E., *Ingratiation*. New York: Appleton-Century-Crofts, 1964.

Jones, E. E., and Gerard, H. B., *Foundations of social psychology*, New York: Wiley, 1967.

Katz, E., and Lazarsfeld, P. F., *Personal influence: the part played by people in the flow of mass communications*. New York: Free Press, 1955.

Kelley, H. H., Communication in experimentally created hierarchies. *Human Relations,* 1951, **4**, 39-56.

Kelley, H. H., Two functions of reference groups. In G. E. Swanson, T. M. Newcomb, and E. L. Hartley (Eds.), *Readings in social psychology*. New York: Holt, Rinehart, and Winston, 2nd edition, 1952.

Kelman, H. C., Compliance, identification, and internalization. *Journal of Conflict Resolution,* 1958, **2**, 51-60.

Kelman, H. C., and Eagly, A. H., Attitude toward the communicator, perception of communication content and attitude change. *Journal of Personality and Social Psychology,* 1965, **1**, 63-78.

Kiesler, C. A., Group pressure and conformity. In J. Mills (Ed.), *Advanced experimental social psychology*. New York: Macmillan, 1969.

Kiesler, C. A., and Corbin, L. H., Commitment, attraction, and conformity, *Journal of Personality and Social Psychology,* 1965, **2**, 890-895.

Kiesler, C. A., and De Salvo, J., The group as an influencing agent in a forced compliance paradigm. *Journal of Experimental Social Psychology,* 1967, **3**, 160-171.

Kiesler, C. A., Kiesler, S. B., and Pallak, M. S., The effect of commitment to future interaction on reactions to norm violations. *Journal of Personality,* 1967, **35**, 585-599.

Kiesler, C. A., Zanna, M., and Nisbett, R. E., On inferring one's beliefs from one's behavior. Unpublished manuscript, 1968.

Kiesler, C. A., Zanna, M., and De Salvo, J., Deviation and conformity: opinion change as a function of commitment, attraction, and presence of a deviate. *Journal of Personality and Social Psychology,* 1966, **3**, 458-467.

Kinsey, A. C., Pomeroy, W. B., and Martin, C. E., *Sexual behavior in the human male.* Philadelphia: Saunders, 1948.

Kogan, N., and Wallach, M. A., Effects of physical separation of group members upon group risk-taking. *Human Relations,* 1967, **20**, 41-48.

Krech, D., Crutchfield, R. S., and Ballachey, E. L., *Individual in society.* New York: McGraw-Hill, 1962.

League, B. J., and Jackson, D. N., Conformity, veridicality, and self-esteem. *Journal of Personality and Social Psychology,* 1964, **68**, 113-115.

Lewin, K., *Resolving social conflicts.* New York: Harper, 1948.

Lippitt, R., Polansky, N., Redl, F., and Rosen, S., The dynamics of power. *Human Relations,* 1952, **5**, 37-64.

Medow, H., and Zander, A., Aspirations for the group chosen by central and peripheral members. *Journal of Personality and Social Psychology,* 1965, **1**, 224-228.

Milgram, S., Behavioral study of obedience. *Journal of Abnormal and Social Psychology,* 1963, **67**, 371-378.

Milgram, S., Some conditions of obedience and disobedience to authority. In I. D. Steiner and M. Fishbein (Eds.), *Current studies in social psychology.* New York: Holt, Rinehart, and Winston, 1965, pp. 243-262.

Orne, M. T., On the social psychology of the psychological experiment: With particular reference to demand characteristics and their implications. *American Psychologist,* 1962, **17**, 776-783.

Ostrom, T. M., and Upshaw, H. S., Psychological perspective and attitude change. In A. G. Greenwald, T. C. Brock, and T. M. Ostrom, *Psychological foundations of attitudes.* New York: Academic Press, 1968.

Pepitone, A. Motivational effects in social perception. *Human Relations,* 1950, **3**, 57-76.

Raven, B. H., and Rietsema, J., The effects of varied clarity of group goal and group path upon the individual and his relation to the group. *Human Relations,* 1957, **10**, 29-44.

Rohrer, J. H., Baron, S. H., Hoffman, E. L., and Swander, D. V., The stability of autokinetic judgments. *Journal of Abnormal and Social Psychology,* 1954, **49**, 595-597.

Rosenberg, M. J., When dissonance fails: On eliminating evaluation apprehension from attitude measurement. *Journal of Personality and Social Psychology,* 1965, **1**, 28-43.

Rosenthal, R., On the social psychology of the psychological experiment: The experimenter's hypothesis as an unintended determinant of experimental results. *American Scientist,* 1963, **51**, 268-283.

Schachter, S., Deviation, rejection, and communication. *Journal of Abnormal and Social Psychology,* 1951, **46**, 190-207.

Schachter, S., Ellertson, N., McBride, D., and Gregory, D., An experimental study of cohesiveness and productivity. *Human Relations,* 1951, **4**, 229-238.

Schein, E. H., Reaction patterns to severe, chronic stress in American army prisoners of war of the Chinese. *Journal of Social Issues,* 1957, **13**, 21-30.

Secord, P. F., and Backman, C. W., *Social psychology.* New York: McGraw-Hill, 1964.

Sherif, M., A study of some social factors in perception. *Archives of Psychology,* 1935, **27**, No. 187.

Siegel, A. E., and Siegel, S., Reference groups, membership groups, and attitude change. *Journal of Abnormal and Social Psychology,* 1957, **55**, 360-364.

Singer, J. E., Brush, C. A., and Lublin, S. C., Some aspects of deindividuation: Identification and conformity. *Journal of Experimental Social Psychology,* 1965, **1**, 365-378.

Strickland, L. H., Surveillance and trust. *Journal of Personality,* 1958, **26**, 200-215.

Thibaut, J. W., and Kelley, H. H., *The social psychology of groups.* New York: Wiley, 1959.

Thibaut, J. W., and Riecken, H. W., Some determinants and consequences of the perception of social causality. *Journal of Personality,* 1955, **24**, 113-133.

Thomas, E. J., Effects of facilitative role inter-dependence on group functioning. *Human Relations,* 1957, **10**, 347-366.

Thrasher, F., *The gang.* Chicago: University of Chicago Press, 1927.

Tsouderos, J., Organizational change in terms of a series of selected variables. *American Sociological Review,* 1955, **20**, 207-210.

White, R., and Lippitt, R., Leader behavior and member reaction in three "social climates." In D. Cartwright, and A. Zander (Eds.), *Group dynamics.* New York: Harper and Row, 3rd edition, 1968, pp. 318-335.

Whyte, W. F., *Street corner society: The social structure of an Italian slum.* Chicago: University of Chicago Press, 1943.

Wolff, R., The value of member contributions as determinant of attraction to a group. Unpublished Ph.D. dissertation, University of Michigan, 1953.

Zimbardo, P. G., and Ebbesen, E., *Influencing Attitudes and Changing Behavior.* Reading, Mass.: Addison-Wesley, to be published in 1969.

ABCDE69